Dedicated to our students—
past, present, and future

Writing and Research in Religious Studies

DONALD E. MILLER
University of Southern California

BARRY JAY SELTSER
Social Issues Research

PRENTICE HALL, Englewood Cliffs, New Jersey 07632

Library of Congress Cataloging-in-Publication Data

Writing and research in religious studies / by Donald E. Miller, Barry
  Jay Seltser.
      p.   cm.
    Includes index.
    ISBN 0-13-971078-7
    1. Religion—Study and teaching (Higher)—United States.
  I. Miller, Donald Earl.   II. Seltser, Barry Jay.
  BL41.W75 1992
  291'.07—dc20   90-47786
                                                                CIP

Editorial/production supervision and
  interior design: Patricia V. Amoroso
Cover design: NSG Designs
Prepress buyer: Herb Klein
Manufacturing buyers: David Dickey and Patrice Fraccio
Acquisitions editor: Ted Bolen

Printed in the United States of America

10 9 8 7 6 5 4 3 2 1

The views expressed in this book do not represent those of the United
States General Accounting Office (GAO), and all of the work for this
book was done before Barry Jay Seltser's employment with the GAO.

ISBN 0-13-971078-7

PRENTICE HALL INTERNATIONAL (UK) LIMITED, *London*
PRENTICE-HALL OF AUSTRALIA PTY. LIMITED, *Sydney*
PRENTICE-HALL CANADA INC., *Toronto*
PRENTICE-HALL HISPANOAMERICANA, S.A., *Mexico*
PRENTICE-HALL OF INDIA PRIVATE LIMITED, *New Delhi*
PRENTICE-HALL OF JAPAN, INC., *Tokyo*
SIMON & SCHUSTER ASIA PTE. LTD., *Singapore*
EDITORA PRENTICE-HALL DO BRASIL, LTDA., *Rio de Janeiro*

Writing and Research in Religious Studies

Contents

7 Elements of Participant Observation: An Overview 46

8 What to Look For 55

9 Interviewing 70

10 Analyzing the Data 81

section four
WRITING YOUR PAPER

11   Getting Started   *90*

12   Writing Style   *97*

13   Documenting Your Sources   *104*

14   Formatting and Editing Your Paper   *114*

APPENDICES

1   Membership in Religious Organizations   *125*

2   Using Computers for Analysis   *129*

Note to Instructors

This book is written primarily for use in undergraduate courses in religious studies in which students are expected to write an extensive research paper. Although such courses are usually found in religious studies departments, this text may also be useful in certain sociology or research methodology courses.

We focus on both library research and on what is usually called "qualitative" field research methods. We expect that some courses will not involve empirical research; in such cases, Section Three can be ignored by your students. Likewise, if students are assigned projects that exclusively require field research, Section Two on library research may not be relevant.

Our rationale for including sections on both library and field research is that an increasing number of professors have discovered the value of requiring students to use the community surrounding their college or university as a laboratory for observing religious practice. Assignments vary from having students attend several services of different religious groups to requiring term-long projects in which students study in depth a single religious setting. While all religion professors are conversant with library research, many humanities faculty members are less comfortable offering advice about field research methodology. Consequently, in addition to providing students with a guide to doing library research, we have given detailed instructions on how to select a religious setting and how to do participant observation research, including writing field notes, conducting interviews with clergy and members, and analyzing field notes.

We suggest assigning this book within the first few weeks of your course. It is written in a style that requires little classroom discussion. Once you have given the term project assignment, students will probably find that this book answers most of their questions about how to select a topic, find resources for their project in the library, take notes, outline their paper, document sources, prepare a bibliography, and so on. We have also dealt with some of the most common writing problems that students have.

We recognize, however, that there is no substitute for a careful reading of a draft by the instructor. Therefore, we strongly recommend that you consider offering to read the first drafts of your students' papers, or at least to review the outlines before they begin the drafting process. In this manner, you (or a teaching assistant) can help the students who are having problems with organization or thematic development.

This book is intended to be a supplement to other course texts, lectures, and class discussion. In particular, you will not find any historical accounts of the development of religion, any descriptive comparisons of the demographics of different religious groups, or very much theoretical discussion. We trust that other books can provide such information. Our task is to help your students think about and conduct research; it is up to you to provide the content and context for the study of religion. Section One of the book, however, does introduce students to a number of terms and concepts commonly used in religious studies, therefore making this an appropriate book to use at the beginning of your course.

We have written for a fairly broad common denominator of undergraduate students and course projects. We expect that you will have some specific guidelines for the papers as well, and the book tells the student to follow your advice when and if it should conflict with ours. On occasion, we suggest that students might seek you out for further advice on a difficult point (such as dealing with anxiety at the beginning of the study). But the book includes sufficient information to allow most students to work from start to finish on their own, without much additional consultation or information necessary on your part.

ACKNOWLEDGMENTS

This book has emerged out of our interaction with students over a period of almost two decades of teaching introductory courses in religious studies. Therefore, we want to thank our students for raising many of the questions that this book attempts to answer. We have also received valuable advice from the following individuals who reviewed earlier drafts of this manuscript, and we are grateful for their suggestions: Wade Clark Roof, University of California,

Santa Barbara; James E. Gibson, Temple University; Robert C. Monk, McMurry College; and Betty Bamberg, University of Southern California. A doctoral student in the School of Religion at USC, Michael McKenzie, prepared the index for the book, and we appreciate his assistance in this regard. Finally, we are most appreciative of the collegial relationship that we have had with a number of individuals at Prentice Hall, including Ted Bolen, Pattie Amoroso, and Caroline Carney.

DONALD E. MILLER

BARRY JAY SELTSER

Writing and Research
in Religious Studies

1

Introduction: Coping with Your Research Project Assignment

Many students approach their research project assignment with mixed feelings. Some of you may never have written an extended paper, and therefore you have considerable anxiety about the prospect of spending an entire semester or quarter on one paper. Others of you may know exactly what you want to write about, but resent the fact that references and bibliography have to be done in a particular way (which you can never quite remember). Still others of you have already calculated that this is one assignment that you can delay until the final weeks of the course.

These feelings of anxiety and resentment, as well as the human tendency toward proscrastination, are real. Research and writing are hard work. Indeed, if your professor has given you a challenging assignment, it may be among the most difficult things you will be doing in the next few months. Studying for an exam or taking lecture notes is relatively easy compared to writing a good research paper.

It is also possible, however, for this project to be the most rewarding thing you will do this term. The very fact that this assignment deals with religion means that you have the opportunity to address questions related to how individuals find meaning in their lives, make value judgments, and form communities centered on creating a good life and a good society. Whether or not you are personally religious should have little bearing on your potential enjoyment of a term project in religious studies, although it may have some bearing on the specific project that interests you.

Your enjoyment of the term project assignment you have been given will depend, in large part, on how you approach the task. While you may resist taking several hours to read a book on writing and research in religious studies, we are confident of the following:

- Spending several hours at the beginning of your project reading this text will potentially save you many hours of "fumbling time" later on;
- Once you have a plan for your project, you can settle into enjoying the process of researching and writing your paper; and
- What you learn in doing this paper will transfer to many other term project assignments you may encounter.

A term research project, if done correctly, can be an enormously creative activity. Even a freshman-level project can produce original research. If a research paper is well done, your instructor will enjoy reading it and will learn from it. At the same time, a poorly done research paper will be boring for you and tedious for your professor to read. The intent of this book is to provide you with the tools to enable you to carefully research a topic and then write a paper that invites your instructor to attend to its content rather than be alienated by the form in which it is presented.

This is a very practical book. Section One introduces you to major terms and concepts in religious studies and then deals with how to choose a research topic. Section Two focuses on library research: how to find sources within your own college or university library and how to read and take notes from these sources. Section Three is intended for those of you whose assignment requires field research. Very specific ideas are given for how to select a religious setting, what is involved in participant observer research, how to interview clergy and members, and how to analyze the data you collect in your observational experiences and interviews. Section Four deals with the actual task of writing, documenting your sources, and outlining and formatting your paper. We have also supplied several appendices that may be helpful. Appendix 1 lists the membership figures for several religious organizations in the United States. For those of you engaging in field research, Appendix 2 tells you some of the advantages of using a computer for recording your field research notes as well as transcribing your interviews. And Appendix 3 provides some examples of sample field notes, for those of you doing field research.

For starters, we suggest that you spend an hour or so of your time skimming through the entire book. Having done this, you should then reread specific sections of the book as they are appropriate to the stage of research in which you are engaged. We do have one warning, however: Don't skip the last section, "Writing Your Paper." While these chapters may seem like a rehash of what you have learned in your freshman composition course, *form* and *content* are of equal importance in a research paper. How you organize your paper and the care with which you attend to details such as headings, references, and sentence structure all contribute to how well you will communicate the results of your research.

Independent research is a skill to be learned, and it is quite different from the ability to read a textbook or take lecture notes. Hence, you should not think of a research paper as an assignment that your professor has "tacked on" to the course. Lectures and textbooks provide you information in a digested and packaged form. Your professor and the authors of your textbooks have already done the hard work of sifting and organizing what is important for you to learn. The purpose of a research paper, howoever, is for you to dig around in primary sources (whether they be texts, or places you visit or people you interview) and then do your own analysis.

In a research paper, no one is going to tell you what your conclusions should be. And the frightening part of doing research is that you have to decide on the limits and extent of your research. Every research project has parallels to taking a trip to a new place; you may have some maps to follow and a fellow traveler (your professor) who has been there before, but the trip and itinerary are yours to plan, and the voyage is yours to take.

In the next chapter, we provide you with a basic vocabulary—what you might think of as a traveling dictionary of terms—that will make your journey into researching a topic in religious studies a bit easier.

section one
THE NATURE OF RESEARCH
IN RELIGION

2

A Brief Overview
of the Nature
# of Religion

This book is not intended to replace the lectures or reading materials from your course, which will provide you with an understanding of the nature, function, and diversity of religion as a human institution and experience. But it might be helpful to point to a few of the crucial features in religious phenomena, in order to help you begin to recognize what *kind* of thing you are studying and to aid you in beginning to develop some ideas for your paper topics.

RELIGION, CULTURE, AND MEANING

Religion is a crucial part of what is often called human culture, a term referring to the total context of symbols, images, and concepts that structure our sense of the world. Books, music, paintings, political ideas; marriages, funerals; school systems, social clubs—all are part and parcel of our culture. The purpose of such diverse elements is to help us make sense of our world, to live in it as creative and productive people, and to understand how and why we live and what our lives are for.

Religion, as part of culture, is also deeply concerned with questions of "making sense" and "meaning." Because of this, the study of religion is likely to require the same interpretive techniques we use in examining and understanding other aspects of culture. Religion can be looked at from the outside—

we can count people who attend church, we can describe the shape of religious buildings, we can list the names of gods and devils that are worshipped or feared. But doing this cannot provide us with a very full or rich understanding of the purpose of religion, which is to speak to people at a deeper level. Therefore, we need to look at religion from the *inside*, asking about the inner experiences of the believer, searching for the meanings provided by religious symbols, looking for the interpretations given to the words and sounds and shapes that we find.

THE SACRED

The particular focus of the religious aspect of culture is centered on the notion of the *sacred*. In whatever form it may take, religions are concerned in particular with establishing and defining a sphere of the "sacred." This term is usually used as a way of distinguishing the religious dimension from the more everyday and common realm of our experience, referred to by the term *profane*. The profane is the world in which we live most of our lives—in it, things are generally what they seem, the rules are clear, and we are essentially in control, if not as individuals, then at least as groups of people.

But the sacred is a realm of experience that is, by definition, "other." It is, first of all, set apart, distinguishable, recognizable to anyone who is a member of the society. But its quality as being set apart is defined not merely by being *other*, but also by the power and feelings that are generated in its presence. These are feelings of specialness, of wonder, of awe, of a sense that, somehow, something strange and out of our common knowledge and control is breaking through into our life.

One of the most famous discussions of religion speaks of the radical otherness and radical power of the sacred by focusing on the meaning of the term *holy*, a word that is usually synonymous with the word *sacred*. Rudolf Otto, writing early in this century, used the word *numinous* to express the radically other and mysterious aspect of the holy. In an evocative phrase, he spoke of the "mysterium tremendum et fascinosum" to describe what people experience when they refer to the holy; a realm of tremendous and fascinating mystery, a radically other sort of experience that conjures up deep emotions as diverse as fear, amazement, fascination, powerlessness, humility, and urgency in the person who is confronted by the experience.[1]

It is worth noting that religious communities are not the sole contexts for experiencing what people have come to call the sacred realm of human life. For many, the experience of personal love has a sacred quality about it—the powerful feelings of being "swept away," the glorious awareness of seeing in someone qualities that one never thought possible, the revelation that one can in fact be loved by another. Similarly, great art can create a sense that one has

---

[1] Rudolf Otto, *The Idea of the Holy*, 2nd edition (London: Oxford University Press, 1950).

been gripped by a power beyond all understanding; listening to a Beethoven quartet or a Bach Mass, for example, can make us feel the same sort of awe, wonder, and amazement.

But religions are particularly concerned with this realm of human experience. Indeed, religious institutions can be seen as the settings within which the sacred can be experienced, protected, and structured. Religions can do this in various ways, all of which are particularly important for understanding the function of religious life. Let's examine a few of the methods by which religious traditions are able to respond to, foster, and provide a context for the experience of the sacred dimension of human existence.

First, religions can create **sacred space**. A temple, church, shrine, mountain, river—any physical place can be identified as the particular spot into which that other dimension is poured out into the world, and from which we can participate in that experience. When we step into that space, in other words, we are, in some odd way, actually leaving one world and entering another, however "close" we may still be to our old world. Indeed, a space can be profane at some times and sacred at others; for example, when a new religious building is "consecrated," it is changed from a building with walls and a roof into a place for the sacred to enter and reside.

Second, religions create **sacred time**. During a religious worship service, for example, the minutes continue to pass, but the significance of time has been radically (if subtly) altered. Similarly, religious holidays (a term literally meaning "holy days") establish a wholly new order of the calendar, in which what is important is not that September follows August but that the harvest has been brought forth as a symbol of a god's love of the world. For example, the Jewish Sabbath is perceived as a holy day set apart from all others, within which God's presence and relationship with the community is focused upon and enlivened. Such holy days both commemorate events that have gone before, and provide a context for a renewed and renewing reimmersion of the believer into the wider context of the sacred. Similarly, in traditions such as Buddhism, one of the purposes of meditation and prayer is to lift the individual out of the everyday awareness of the passage of time, to a plane where one is linked up with the "eternal" or the "timeless."

Third, religions usually create **sacred language**. In some cases, a wholly different linguistic system is used for religious worship, such as the traditional use of Hebrew in Jewish services or the traditional use of Latin in Roman Catholic services in the past. But even if the same everyday language is spoken, it is likely to take on radically different meanings and resonances when conducted in sacred time and sacred space. Phrases become infused with sacred significance when spoken in certain ritual contexts, or when associated with particular religious texts. For example, the phrase "the kingdom and the power and the glory for ever and ever" is perfectly good and normal English, but virtually drips with religious meaning for anyone who has ever been exposed to what Christians refer to as the Lord's Prayer. In addition, the pace and richness of religious language set it apart from our everyday speech patterns; prayers, sermons, even the way in which people greet each other in religious contexts—all these forms of speech are likely to be much more poetic, metaphorical, and refer to something beyond their "literal" meaning.

Fourth, religions create and are nourished by **sacred objects and activities**. Anything can become defined in this way—books (such as the Bible or the Koran), dances (such as the Shaker rituals), features of nature (rivers), human artifacts (crosses or statues). Whether or not the object is made by persons, it is created *as* sacred when a religious community assigns such meaning to it (or, to put it more in the language of the community, when they acknowledge its inherently sacred quality).

Fifth, religions can create **sacred feelings**. We can feel awe in looking at a beautiful sunset or listening to a moving sonata; it is the task of the religious mind to interpret such awe in terms of the sacred nature of beauty and harmony. The experience, in other words, is changed, so that it is seen not just as a feeling of awe, but as one of awe leading (for example) to gratitude for a god who has created such beauty, or to a sense of the smallness and finitude of all human endeavors. Whatever the particular interpretation, such experiences, when brought into a religious context, are seen as pointing to the sacred, to the wholly other, which somehow shapes and undergirds our everyday life.

MYTH

Religions often encapsulate their understanding of the sacred in what are termed *sacred myths*. In modern English, the word *myth* has come to mean a story that is not true, as in the phrase "That's only a myth." But, in religious terms, a myth is any powerful and evocative story that dramatically reveals something about the underlying meaning and purpose of creation, nature, or history. Myths are the oldest forms of religious reflection, usually passed on orally from generation to generation, and providing the central themes for a culture's self-understanding and self-definition.

Myths are particularly important because they help us to figure out who we are and how we came to be. Creation myths provide images about the origins of the universe and the human race; communal myths give insights into our society's beliefs about its role in the wider history of the human race. The proper question to ask about a myth is not whether it is true, but whether (and how) it reveals something fundamental about a community's sense of the meaning of its own existence and that of the wider world of which it is a part.

Myths become sacred when they deal with the realm of human experience that is perceived to be in contact with something beyond itself—something powerful, fundamental, creative, and unknowable. In most situations, they involve recounting the moments and places where the sacred somehow has "made contact" with the everyday, where people believe that they have glimpsed (however briefly and tentatively) something of the fundamental nature of reality. Different religious traditions speak in different words about such moments, but they share a common view that such moments are special, worthy of being preserved, and point to the deepest truths about life and existence. It is not surprising, therefore, that these myths become the most influential and powerful stories any culture tells about itself.

The precise "content" of the sacred or holy can vary, of course. Indeed, the differences provide one important way to distinguish between conflicting religious traditions and movements. For some religions, there is a "deity" of some sort that is the focus of worship or thought about the sacred—for example, God, Allah, Lord Krishna. In other traditions, the sacred is found in a more impersonal idea (such as Nirvana in Buddhism). For others, the focus is on a concept that may resemble a philosophical idea more than an explicitly spiritual entity— for example, "Jen" in Confucianism or "The Tao" in Taoism. For some religions, there are many different sacred entities, as in the case of polytheistic traditions such as Hinduism and much so-called primitive religion.

Precisely because the sacred is not simply another object or idea as part of our everyday lives, religions usually have to refer to the sacred realm by indirection. The names themselves are generally seen to point to the sacred, rather than capturing it entirely; for example, in traditional Judaism, the name of God is not spoken, and the specific pronunciation of the name is no longer known. The same point is captured in the famous Taoist passage: "The Tao that can be told of is not the Absolute Tao; The Names that can be given are not absolute Names."[2]

SYMBOLS

As we have already suggested, religious groups use various images or signs with which to point to the sacred—not to capture or control it, necessarily, but to indicate its presence and suggest some of its qualities. Such pointers are *symbols*, and can take the form of words, physical objects, sounds, or actions. A symbol is something that represents and evokes a significant aspect of the culture of which it is a part. Symbols can be objects (a wooden cross), sounds (a hymn or a mantra), or actions (bowing down or kneeling at prayer). Whatever its form, the power of a symbol lies in its ability to point to something meaningful in the lives and experiences of the community in which it is found.

Although we find symbols in all arenas of our lives, they are especially crucial in religious systems. Precisely because religion seeks to point beyond the everyday world to a sacred realm, symbols become essential in directing

---

[2] *Tao Te Ching*; quoted in Roger Schmidt, *Exploring Religion* (California: Wadsworth, 1980), p. 69.

our gaze and attention toward that other realm, and in ordering and interpreting the experience of that sacred realm.

In your research, whatever the specific topic, you will need to focus on the relevant symbols that are found in the tradition you are studying, and ask about their meaning and significance to the people who relate to them. Indeed, it is not an exaggeration to say that most of the work you will be doing will involve identifying, understanding, and explaining the roles of various symbols in the life of religious communities, individuals, or theories you are examining.

There are several ways to categorize different types of symbols, a few of which are presented here:

1. As already noted, symbols can come in different forms, such as objects, sounds, or actions. Symbols of various sorts can all point to the same underlying image or feeling; at the same time, a single symbol may in fact "symbolize" various important aspects of the religious culture.

2. Symbols can be natural or manufactured. Rivers, mountains, trees, the sky, the sun—all of these are symbols in different religious traditions. Human-made objects or sounds can also function as symbols, of course. In some cases, the two types of symbols even merge, as in the case of the cross, which is often referred to as a tree.

3. Each religious tradition has central and peripheral symbols. Although there is no clear line to draw between them, it is always important to try to identify which symbols function as the pivotal and crucial ones for a religious community. The placement of an object at a central spot in the sacred space, or its use or evocation at a crucial moment of sacred time, may be a good indication of its importance. In addition, references to the symbol in other sacred contexts (such as in religious writings or in song) may point to the significance of the particular symbol.

4. Symbols can be public or private.[3] Public symbols are the expressed links between individuals and their religious communities, perceptible to anyone who participates in the sacred space or time of that community. Private symbols may be communicated, but their meaning is focused in the more internal consciousness of a particular person. Dreams, places we have visited, memories of time spent with a loved one, can all be personal symbols that resonate as powerfully for each of us as the more public and shared images which the community presents to us.

In studying and analyzing a religious movement or tradition, your task is made both easier and harder by the existence of such symbols. It is easier, because the symbols provide some hints about what people

---

[3] This distinction is drawn from Kenneth Boulding, and is referred to in Robert Ellwood's book *Introducing Religion* (Englewood Cliffs, N.J.: Prentice Hall, 1978), p. 105.

believe and what their understanding of the sacred is. Without symbols, religion would consist of silence in the face of the complete mystery and otherness of the sacred. Indeed, one way to acknowledge the necessity of symbols is to recognize that such silence would itself be a symbol of precisely that mystery and otherness! If a community is to position itself in relation to the sacred, and to define its life and activity in the light of its own understanding of the sacred (however it might be understood), some sorts of pointers must be used, or else there is nothing to say, do, think, believe, or live by.

But symbols also complicate the process of our understanding, precisely because they are, of necessity, *ambiguous*. Because a symbol is not in fact the object or idea being represented, it can be interpreted in a variety of ways, and one must struggle to figure out precisely what is being symbolized. For example, Buddhists have a symbol of a seated figure, who is often used as the focus for meditation.

What does such a seated figure represent? There are numerous possibilities, of course, including rest and relaxation; readiness to stand up or lie down; conversation with someone else who is also seated; or some features or attributes of the seated figure himself. Just by looking at the figure, one would not automatically know what was being represented, and therefore what the believer is made mindful of when looking at the symbol.

To take a more familiar example in American society, the Cross is a central symbol for the Christian faith—but what, precisely, does it represent?

Again, there are many possibilities, which increase the more one studies and learns about the history and theology of the Christian tradition. The Cross can represent death, suffering, self-sacrifice, God's becoming human, the love of one person for all others, or a host of other images or ideals. As an insider, many or all of these meanings may be conjured up at once; in fact, part of the power of a symbol lies in its ability to represent many such religious ideals and feelings.

Your task in studying religious symbols is to figure out what these symbols mean to people within a particular religious community or tradition, and to ask why these particular symbols are appropriate to represent those particular values or ideals. Once again, your work must involve an empathetic effort to put yourself imaginatively inside the heart, mind, and soul of the members of the community, and to sense what it would be like to use that symbol to represent the sacred.

Because the sacred is the realm of mystery and incomprehensibility, it is not surprising that some traditions emphasize the fact that *no* symbols can adequately represent what is being worshipped and adored. In Orthodox Judaism and Islam, for example, no visual symbols are allowed to refer to the ultimate power of the universe, for fear that believers will confuse the physical and limited symbol with what is being symbolized. (It is precisely because of this fear that idolatry is considered one of the greatest evils by these religious traditions.) What is important to realize, however, is that, from the standpoint of the observer, the refusal to allow such symbols is itself a crucial symbol, representing the belief that the divine is thoroughly "other" and out of human control and understanding.

One of the most important assumptions you should bring into the research is that *anything* is potentially a religious symbol. This is why it is so important to open all your senses (hearing, seeing, tasting, touching, smelling) and your imagination to what is going on around you, whether you are observing a worship service, interviewing a religious person about her faith, reading a religious document, or struggling to understand the historical development of a doctrine or practice. No object, feeling, or activity is inherently profane or inherently sacred; it is the community's interpretation that makes them so, and your task is to understand how that process comes about and what its significance is for the people for whom those objects, feelings, or activities are holy.

3
Choosing Your Topic

Autobiographical descriptions of the experience of prayer, historical accounts of the development of a religious tradition, and your own observations and interviews are the types of information that constitute the ingredients for a research paper. But the final product depends on a recipe that tells you what to do with them. If you are cooking something, you don't go out and buy the ingredients before deciding on the recipe. Similarly, if you collect all your information before thinking about the organization and analysis, you will just end up with a bunch of disconnected facts and opinions rather than the basis for a coherent paper. Therefore, you should begin your paper with a broad plan in mind, both regarding the goals of the research as well as the methods necessary for accomplishing it.

Ideally, any author should have an outline of what the finished product will look like before beginning the research. But this is seldom possible, or even desirable, in conducting the sort of research project we are considering. It is likely that you will find out something from reading, observing, or interviewing that you might not have predicted, and this new fact or interpretation will become the basis for your paper. There is nothing wrong with this if it happens; indeed, you will probably feel better about the result if you learned something unexpected.

But the opposite extreme is equally unsatisfactory—namely, to conduct your research without any coherent set of ideas, questions, or analysis. Religious institutions are highly complex, meaning that there are numerous topics and themes you could choose to focus on. If you begin your research with a totally open mind (meaning a totally empty one), you will simply founder in a sea of separate experiences and facts.

The solution, of course, is some sort of middle road between a completely structured, predetermined outline and a blank slate. To find this middle ground, we suggest that, before beginning any of your actual research, you sit down and answer the following three questions:

1. What is the main **theme** you wish to focus on?

2. What are the central two or three **questions** you want to ask about this theme?

3. What is the **required information** you will need to answer these questions?

At this stage of the research, your answers to these questions should reflect whatever reading or lecture notes are pertinent but should be influenced mainly by your *interests*. What themes and questions excite you? What would you really like to know about, to spend some time studying and writing about? What kinds of issues would you like to be struggling with over the next couple of months?

The answers you give to these three questions now may bear little or no resemblance to your final paper, but don't worry about that. The point is to find a focus with which to begin your research. Although we do not think it is a good idea to study a group in which you have membership, we do believe that personal experiences and issues often enter into research project decisions. For example, you may be dating someone from a different religious tradition than your own and see this term project as an opportunity to learn something about their religious heritage. Or you may have experienced the death of someone important to you and wondered how a good God who is all powerful can allow human tragedy, which might lead you to investigate the problem of theodicy. Alternatively, you may have seen on television a group who speaks in tongues or believes in faith healing, and decided you would like to visit such a group.

The next section provides you with some ideas for answering the three preliminary questions just cited.

THEMES

A theme is any concept or issue that is raised by a particular research setting or situation. Since you are studying religious institutions, appropriate themes must "fit" this type of organization. Your instructor might suggest (or even limit you to) particular themes that you should use as the focus of your research. We mention some different themes here to give you some ideas:

> The authority structure in Pentecostal churches
>
> The role of the Koran in the everyday life of a Muslim
>
> The nature of membership in a Buddhist temple
>
> The views of Orthodox and Conservative Jews toward abortion
>
> The religious experience of chanting for Hare Krishnas
>
> The importance of the family to Mormons

We could go on and on, but you get the basic idea. A theme is by its nature a broad topic; your theme should be of interest to you and relevant to the sort of organization you are going to study.

QUESTIONS

After choosing a theme, ask a couple of central questions about it. This will probably be easy to do if you have chosen the theme because you are interested in it. In fact, if you cannot quickly generate several interesting questions about the theme, you should pick a different theme.

Examples of questions for each of the themes we just identified are as follows:

Authority structure of the religious group:

1. How are the leaders chosen?
2. Can women hold positions of leadership?
3. Are rules formalized in a code, or are they understood informally?

Role of the Koran in the everyday life of a Muslim:

1. In what ways is the Koran used to determine what people believe and do?
2. How is the Koran used in actual worship services?
3. What parts of the Koran are most central for the members of this group?

Nature of membership in the group:

1. Why do members choose to become active?
2. How does the group try to find new members?
3. In what way does the group function as a "community" for members?

Views of Orthodox and Conservative Jews toward abortion:

1. What are the theological teachings of the groups about abortion?

2. What would the groups' attitude be toward a member who decided to get an abortion?

3. Are the groups involved in lobbying *for* or *against* abortion legislation?

Experience of chanting:

1. Is there a difference between chanting done in public and that done in the private worship of group members?

2. Do members experience "religious ecstasy" while chanting?

3. Does chanting promote group cohesion among members?

Importance of family:

1. What rituals and activities express the importance of the family for group members?

2. What is the theological rationale for emphasizing the role of the family?

3. Is the stress on the family an important recruitment tool for getting others to join?

As you can see, a single theme can generate many different types of questions. Just as you should select a theme that interests you, try to pick those questions that are of most interest to you.

A couple of suggestions about phrasing your questions at this initial stage of the research might be helpful. First, be as specific as you can, trying to ask questions that can be answered in a brief study. For example, instead of asking "How is the group structured?" ask "Who are the group's leaders?" Second, pick questions that lend themselves to the sort of question you might ask in an interview. Imagine someone trying to answer your question, and think about ways to phrase it that will make it clear and interesting to someone else.

REQUIRED INFORMATION

Finally, ask yourself what sort of information you would need to answer these questions you have posed. Your answers will be partly dependent upon the type of assignment you are given. In particular, does your instructor expect you to perform some observations or interviews in a particular religious group, or are you expected only to read and think and analyze information about a topic?

At this point, don't think about what the answers might be, but about how you will go about finding those answers. Consider the range of ways in which you might gather information, and ask yourself which of these will help you find an answer to your question. Wherever possible, identify several different ways to answer the question.

Let's take our first example. Suppose you are interested in studying authority structure, and your key questions concern the relative roles of leaders and other members in the decision-making process of a particular religious group. What types of information would help you here? First, there are numerous types of books and articles that might be extremely useful, including accounts written by members of the group, historical assessments of how understandings of authority developed in the past, and empirical studies that examined the viewpoints of members of the group toward this question. If your assignment is to use library resources, you would begin by identifying the types of written materials that would help you answer the question.

If you are asked to perform some empirical field work of your own (or if you decide that such work would be particularly helpful in answering your questions), what sort of information might be useful in addition to library sources? Attendance at religious services probably will not be useful for this particular topic, except as a way to identify some of the leaders. Instead, attendance at some policy meetings (such as a lay committee, a staff meeting, or the board of elders or deacons) would give you some indication of who participates in such decisions. You could start, therefore, by asking a few people what sorts of meetings occur, and whether you could sit in on some of them.

What sorts of interviews might be helpful for answering this question? In addition to asking people about the meetings you could attend, you will want to ask the people in leadership positions how they view their own role and how open they are (or have to be) in taking other people's views into account. Similarly, you would try to interview several members and ask them whether, in fact, they feel that they have any influence on policy decisions. It would be helpful to speak to some active and some inactive members, to see if there are different perceptions.

Finally, is there any other sort of information that might be helpful? In this example, you might seek out some documentary evidence, such as minutes of previous meetings, to develop some historical perspective on how decisions are made and how often such meetings have occurred.

We have identified several different research methods (library research, observation, interviews, documentary reading), and several specific suggestions within each method, for arriving at answers to this question. Of course, the appropriateness of any particular method will depend on the nature of your theme and questions. Usually, however, you will find (if you think about it carefully) that some combination of looking, listening, asking, and reading will be helpful for most of the sorts of research questions you will pose.

FINDING A RELIGION TO STUDY

Your topic might involve a theme that cuts across various religions, or it might focus on a person or movement that calls for a general discussion. But it is likely that, to provide sufficient focus for your project, you will have to limit your research to an examination of one religion, and probably to one subgroup of that tradition.

The diversity of religious groups in any single religious tradition is enormous, and one of your major tasks in whatever paper you write will be to distinguish the group you are focusing on from other related ones. To take just one example, suppose that you are interested in Buddhism and would like to look at this tradition as it has developed in the United States. You will find that there is a wide range of Buddhist religious organizations, including Zen Centers of various descriptions, Tibetan Buddhists (often associated with Chogyam Trungpa), Nichiren Shoshu (which is a new religious movement), and many others. Each of these groups is Buddhist, but they differ significantly in terms of doctrine, style of organization, and the extent to which they have assimilated themselves to more indigenous American culture. Therefore, in identifying one of these groups to study, you will have to learn something, not just about Buddhism but about the distinctive history, beliefs, and practices of this particular version of Buddhism.

Your choice should depend partly on the sort of topic you want to study, of course. For example, one of the central differences between religious traditions concerns the extent to which ritual is primarily cognitive or affective, structured or unstructured, verbalized or internally experienced. Consider, for example, the obvious differences between a "mainstream" Protestant service and a Buddhist meditation center. In the former, one is likely to have a clearly organized structure, spoken (and often sung) prayers and hymns, readings from a sacred book, a sermon that explains (in logical terms) what the religion teaches, and a few moments of silence. By contrast, the Buddist meditation (in a Zen Center, for example) usually involves a group of people sitting (or walking) in silence, attempting to clear their minds of all specific thoughts and ideas in the pursuit of an intangible experience of emptiness or wholeness. If you are particularly interested in looking at the role of written authorities in religious services, a Buddhist congregation would probably be a poor selection.

Appendix 1 provides some figures on the size and nature of some of the major religions. You can find other information in your course texts, your lecture notes, or by looking in a reference book in the library (see Chapter 4).

YOUR INSTRUCTOR AS A RESOURCE

Once you have done your homework in identifying a topic for your research project, we strongly advise you to make an appointment to see your instructor or teaching assistant (TA). Oftentimes they are busy people, and you don't want to waste their time. But they can be an enormous resource to you. We suggest that you tell your professor or TA in a few sentences what steps you have gone through in identifying your project and the specific focus in which you are interested. Ask if they think your topic is too broad or too narrow. Then ask if they have specific suggestions for how to approach the study or books or articles that you should read.

Most faculty and graduate students are "walking bibliographies," and it would be unfortunate not to read an article or book that your instructor or TA thinks is highly relevant to your topic. Also, you will find in most instances that faculty are much more interested in talking with you about your research topic than in answering questions from your textbook or their lecture. Graduate students and faculty are always involved in research projects of their own, and your own keen interest in responsibly investigating a topic or issue will be highly welcomed.

4

Finding Sources in the Library

Written sources of information are usually essential for any research project, even one involving field work. Your college or university library is the best place to find such information, and you can expect to spend many hours there during the research phase of your project. This chapter is designed to help you master this important resource, and to help you make more efficient use of your time.

Before you go to the library, you should begin by sitting down with a piece of paper and listing several key terms or themes that you want to focus upon. (Reread Chapter 3 if you are having trouble finding a topic). Do not feel that your final paper will have to deal only with these issues; this is a starting point for your research, not a rigid set of constraints.

SAMPLE TOPIC LISTINGS

Religious group or tradition to be studied:

[For example: Quakers, Presbyterians, Zen Buddhists, Mormons]

Issues or themes to be addressed:

[For example: silent worship, authority structure, meditation, missionary activity]

Other possible topics:

[For example: fund raising within New Religious Movements, faith healers in urban settings]

Next, using this list and following our recommendations in Chapter 3, write out two or three questions that represent the central issues you wish to address. An example is, "What is the authority of the minister in the Presbyterian church?" "What is distinctive about Quaker ritual practices?" If possible, try to narrow the topic down to a single sentence. Remember that the more focused your subject, the easier it will be to find relevant sources and the less time you are likely to spend chasing materials that will not be useful.

USING THE LIBRARY

Your library research should proceed from this initial list and set of questions. To make efficient use of your time, you want to move from the *general* to the *specific* level of inquiry. In other words, your first task is to identify some broad information about your issues, reading a few general articles or sections of books, and then narrow down the topic to identify more detailed discussions of specific themes and questions.

If you are not yet familiar with your library, you would be wise to speak to a librarian about your project. Tell the librarian what you are interested in writing about, and ask for help in locating and using the following: card catalogue, computer online search terminals, periodical indices, and the reference room. Once you know where these are located, you can begin to do your preliminary research. But remember that the librarian is there to help you if you run into any problems or have any further questions as you proceed. Doing research is time-consuming enough without wasting your time on a dead-end search because you were afraid to ask for help. The librarian is paid to be of assistance, so don't be shy. Librarians are highly trained professionals with wide-ranging skills in identifying indices, journals, books, and other resources related to your topic.

REFERENCE MATERIALS

There are several important sorts of library reference materials, described in the following sections.

General Reference Works

The best place to start is with some general articles on your topic. If you know virtually nothing about your group or topic, you might want to look at a general article in a good encyclopedia or reference book. Remember that such volumes are intended *only* to get you started; you should not use them as the central references for your paper. Most of these general books are located in the reference room or a special reading room of the library.

USEFUL REFERENCE BOOKS IN RELIGIOUS STUDIES

Encyclopedia Britannica (start with the middle section, the "Micropaedia," which has articles of moderate length on various topics; see the third section, the "Macropaedia," for more detailed articles)

Encyclopedia Americana

The Oxford Dictionary of the Christian Church

A Religious History of the American People, by Sidney Ahlstrom

International Encyclopedia of the Social Sciences (for articles dealing with sociology or anthropology of religion, in particular)

New Catholic Encyclopedia

Encyclopedia Judaica (for short articles on Judaism)

Encyclopedia of Philosophy (if you are interested in philosophical themes such as the proofs for the existence of God, the problem of evil, or rationality and religion)

Read over some general articles dealing with different aspects of your topic. For example, if you think you would like to write something about the Black Muslims, look under this heading, but also try related topics such as "American religions," "Minorities," and "Race." At this initial stage, you don't want to read extremely carefully or take extensive notes, especially from these sources. Such reference books are useful primarily to help you get some ideas for future searches. Skim the entries, and jot down some key words or issues that strike you as interesting. If you do take more extensive notes, be sure to write down precisely which source you were using and the page numbers from which you have taken the information.

Online Computer Search or Card Catalogue

If your project involves primarily library research, you will want to determine fairly early what sorts of books and articles will be available. If your library has a computerized listing of articles or books, ask the librarian how to use it, and begin by examining the listings under some of your key themes and words. Be sure to find out whether the search process is free, because computer searches can be expensive.

Doing a computer search is usually quite simple, especially if your library allows you to enter the topics yourself. Put in two or three key words of your topic under the "subject" index, and browse through the listing to see what sources are available. You may have to try several different terms or phrases before you find the one that generates the correct list; the best advice (other than consulting the librarian) is to use words that specify your topic very narrowly, and then move to more general topics. In this way, you will save time scrolling through large numbers of irrelevant topics.

For example, if you are looking for sources about the Buddhist experience of meditation, don't start with "Eastern Religion" or "Buddhism." Begin with "Meditation in Buddhism" or "Buddhist Meditation" or "Meditative Techniques." If this initial search doesn't yield any titles, try "Meditation" or "Buddhist Practices."

Look through the list of sources, and identify several titles that appear to be closely related to your own topic. Many computer files will provide a brief summary (an abstract) of each article or book, which will help you decide which ones are likely to be most useful. If you see something that looks interesting, even if it is somewhat off the topic, note it as well; at this point in your research, you may find another subject that you would prefer to write about.

Write down the crucial information for each source on either a separate index card or on a piece of paper set aside as your source list.

Also examine the other subject listings that usually appear at the bottom of the screen. They will suggest alternative search categories that you can use later to try to find additional titles.

If your library does not have a computerized catalogue, you will have to use the card catalogue, which is usually located in a central place in the main area of the library. Ask the librarian how to use it if you have any questions. For most topics, you will want to locate the *Subject* cards, rather than *Author* or *Title* cards. Proceed the same way you would in the computerized search: identify several key terms, look up the entries under each one, and write down the information for particularly interesting titles. Make sure you write down the same information listed above for each reference. Also scan the subject headings at the bottom of each card, and use these terms to guide your future searching.

Card catalogues list only books carried by the library; computer searches

---

**INFORMATION TO COPY ON EACH BOOK OR ARTICLE
THAT YOU WANT TO FIND**

Call Number (Usually located at the top of each entry, but occasionally included on a separate line further down the screen. Be sure to copy it down exactly as it appears; include all "extenders," such as the date of publication if it appears in the same call number section.)

Author (Write down the last name first, since that is the way you will find it on the shelf or in a journal.)

Title

Date of Publication

Journal Name, Volume Number, Date, and Page Numbers (if a journal)

---

may also include periodicals, and some even include titles that are not carried by your library. Again, ask the librarian to assist you in locating the correct file with which to begin your search for titles.

Whether you are using a card catalogue or a computer, don't feel that you have to write down every single title you find. In part, how much you write will depend both upon the nature of your topic and the number of sources you find in your search. If your first several key words yield only three sources, you probably want to write them all down; if they yield thirty, be more selective. Remember that you can always return to the same location and find more titles if you need to do so.

How many titles you write down also depends upon how well you have already defined and focused your topic. The clearer you are on the eventual focus of the paper, the more titles you can write down now, because you will want to examine most of them. If you are at the "exploration" stage, you are better off checking out just a few selected sources, instead of reading several articles on a topic you may end up not writing about. Use your judgment; the key is to be systematic as you proceed, and to use the search process not only to gather information but to help you develop the subject and direction of the paper.

Periodical Indices

In many cases, you may prefer to begin with a few journal articles on your subject. You can use any of the following volumes which list articles related to religion.

IMPORTANT INDICES TO CONSULT

The Religion Index
The Humanities Index
The Social Sciences Index
The Reader's Guide to Periodical Literature

In each case, look up several of the key words, and peruse the titles of the articles listed under that heading. These indices are grouped by year; start with the most recent year, and work your way backwards.

Pick out several article titles that seem to be most relevant or interesting, write down all the information under that listing (including the full citation to the journal), and then proceed to the next key word.

Once again, be selective, and allow yourself to be influenced by the titles you discover in your search. Jot down other topics that you think might be as interesting as the one you began with. If you have been wise enough to begin the search process early in the term, you will have time to experiment with several related topics before finally settling on the one to write about.

In a couple of hours of work, you will probably have a lengthy list of twenty or thirty articles. If you have not found anything, you probably have not looked under the appropriate word, so try to reformulate the topic. For example, if not much is listed under "Leadership," try another related term, such as "Authority" or "Control" or "Organizational Structure." You may have to try several times before you find the topics you want.

You will probably find that certain journals are most useful in providing you with articles. In choosing articles from the indices to look for later, we suggest that you try to focus on the following journals, which are likely to be carried in your library and which are among the most respected journals in the field:

IMPORTANT JOURNALS IN RELGION

Journal for the Scientific Study of Religion

Sociological Analysis

Review of Religious Research

Religious Studies Review

Journal of the American Academy of Religion

[*Note:* This is a brief sampling; there are dozens of journals in religious studies. The first three journals are particularly appropriate if you are doing a field research project.]

Somewhat briefer and more popular articles are often found in the following periodicals:

POPULAR PERIODICALS

Christianity and Crisis
Christian Century
Commonweal
Commentary
National Catholic Reporter

PRIMARY AND SECONDARY SOURCES

In doing your library research, it is important to keep in mind the distinction between *primary* and *secondary* sources. Primary sources are written by the subjects of your research itself, or are documents from the religious community you are studying. Secondary sources are the writings of other people about the community or experience. Diaries, letters, scriptural texts (such as the Bible or the Koran), and autobiographies are generally primary sources; biographies, critical reviews, and historical accounts of a religious community are secondary sources.

Note that the distinction between these two types of sources is not always clear and may depend upon the nature of your topic. For example, if you are examining the writings of Saint Paul, books by great theologians may be considered secondary accounts, as they struggle to interpret and make use of his writings. On the other hand, if you are examining the way in which Christian theologians write about prayer or the Bible, these same accounts become the primary data for your study.

The distinction is important, however, because you want your paper to rely on primary data wherever possible. The reason for this is that secondary data are, by definition, already "once removed" from the actual experience or beliefs you are attempting to describe and interpret, and it is always preferable to base your interpretation on acquaintance with the experience itself rather than only on other accounts of it. (Note the word *only* in this sentence, however; secondary accounts are extremely useful in understanding what the experience means.) This point is true in other areas of our lives as well, of course. We would usually prefer to learn about something directly than from someone who heard about it from someone else.

Depending on the nature of your project, primary sources might not be available. If you are engaged in some observation of your own of a religious community, you are gathering your own primary data, and you will probably want to use the library primarily to examine some secondary sources to provide a richer context for your own conclusions and discussion. If your paper is based solely on library research, it may be more important to try to seek out some primary sources on which to base your paper.

One good way to assure that you are including primary sources is to follow the references in books and articles back to the original accounts. You may not find all the referred-to primary sources in your library, but you probably will be able to locate some of them. A few examples of such a search for primary sources are given here:

a. Accounts of the religious community may refer to passages from a holy book (such as the Bible or the Koran or the Bhagavad Gita) which serve as the basis for the particular belief or practice you are studying. Find a copy of that book, locate the cited passages, and read them to determine precisely what is being said and the context in which they are being discussed. It is especially helpful to "read around" the cited passage—for example, read the entire paragraph (or even the entire chapter if it is short) to determine the context.

b. A historical discussion might refer to the writings of a respected thinker or leader of the religious community, whose views helped shape opinions on your topic. Using the footnotes or bibliography, locate the key passages where that person expresses such views. Once you have found the relevant book, don't just read the passage referred to in your secondary source; look at the index under your topic and see if there are other parts of this more primary source that might help you to understand what this figure's contributions were to your subject.

c. A person you are interviewing or a religious writer you are examining refers to a poem or play or short story that played a major role in shaping his or her perspective. Track down that reference, read through it quickly, and ask yourself why that piece of literature would have had such an effect. In the process of doing this, you may develop a much better sense of the inner meaning and power of the tradition you are studying.

OBTAINING WRITTEN INFORMATION FROM OTHER SOURCES

Although your library is the appropriate place to start, it need not be the only source of written information. You will save yourself a lot of time if you make full use of your own library first, including working with a librarian to make sure you have located everything that is relevant for your project. Depending on your project, however, there are other places you might want to go to get more information, such as the following:

1. Other libraries. Your library probably has an interlibrary loan arrangement with other schools. Ask the librarian to help you locate other libraries that might have particular books you cannot find.

2. Offices of the religious group you are studying. If the group has headquarters or a regional office in your area, make a phone call and ask them if they have any written information on your topic, or whether you could come in and interview someone. Alternatively, write a brief letter to the religious headquarters; you can find the address either in a library reference source (ask your librarian), by calling a local organization (such as a synagogue, mosque, or church) and asking them for the address of their main offices, or by consulting the Yellow Pages of your telephone directory (under "Religion"). In your letter, explain briefly who you are, what your topic is, and request any written documents they may have on your subject. Be sure to provide your address in the letter.

5

Reading
and Taking Notes

Let's assume you have looked through some periodical indices and card catalogues and have assembled a list of fifteen or twenty articles and books on your topic. How do you proceed to look at them, and which ones should you use?

The first thing to remember is our advice about moving from the general to the specific. Look for the ones with the broader titles that seem to address your topic most fully, rather than the ones that have a narrow focus. For example, if your topic concerns the rise of the Hare Krishna movement in the United States, it is better to start by looking for a couple of general historical treatments of new religious movements and the Hare Krishna movement itself, and leave more detailed accounts of the beliefs or practices of the Hare Krishna movement for later. Similarly, if your subject is the prayer life of Reform Jews, begin with some articles or books describing Reform Judaism and the ways Jews pray.

The exception to this rule is if you find a title that seems to address precisely the subject you are trying to study. You will want to look at such sources first, not only because they are likely to be the most helpful, but because you may have to narrow down your subject considerably if you find that much has already been written on that topic. Remember that your paper will be better if it can focus more precisely on a subject about which you can say something significant, rather than on a topic about which you can barely skim the surface in your short paper.

It is helpful to look at this stage of the research process as a continual back-and-forth exercise. Do not approach the search for sources as something that needs to be done once and for all at the beginning; you can, and should, return to the card catalogue, online computer listing, and periodical index several times as you proceed to take notes and develop your topic further. In some cases, this will mean looking for more titles on the same topic; in others, you might need to search out different topics to expand, narrow, or completely alter your original topic.

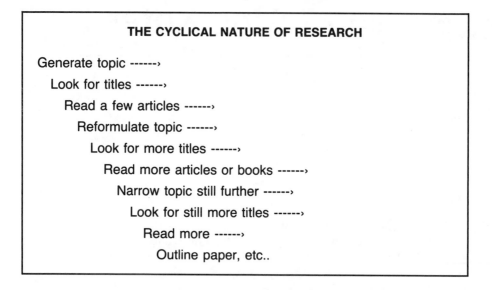

THE CYCLICAL NATURE OF RESEARCH

Generate topic ------›

  Look for titles ------›

    Read a few articles ------›

     Reformulate topic ------›

      Look for more titles ------›

       Read more articles or books ------›

        Narrow topic still further ------›

         Look for still more titles ------›

          Read more ------›

           Outline paper, etc..

The precise order of these steps might be different, and the number of times you go back to search for titles will vary according to the nature of your topic and how well you chose your topic at the beginning.

Do not feel that the need to repeat this process several times is a sign that you are not doing a good job, or that you should have been able to find "the right topic" the first time you tried to do so. Many of the best papers come out of a difficult and time-consuming process of redefinition, dead-end leads, and new beginnings. This is simply one more reason to force yourself to get started early in the semester.

Once you have found a few sources that address the broad nature of your topic, you should begin by skimming through several of these sources. Skimming is best done by looking through the table of contents and the index, locating the sections most relevant for your topic, and then quickly reading through these portions of the source. Once you have found sections in your skimming that are going to be useful for your paper, it is time to begin taking notes.

Reading your sources should be viewed as an interactive process. You are not merely trying to squeeze facts, figures, and opinions out of the writers; you also need to interpret what they are saying and decide how you will use what they are saying. There are several questions you need to ask of any source, whether it is an article, a book, an interview, or a document gathered from a denominational office:

1. *Who is the source?* What particular biases might this person or group bring to the topic? For example, is the writer a member of the community being studied? Was she expelled from the group? How well does she know the group? What academic training (if any) does she have? You might not be able to find out some of this information, but you should be alert to clues and explicit statements in the text that give you some ideas.

2. *Who published the source?* Even if you know little or nothing about the writer, the publisher may give you some information about potential bias. As a general rule, documents issued by organizations themselves tend to make them look good, so it is less likely that you are getting a purely "objective" account. This does *not* mean that you should avoid or discount such sources, merely that you want to balance them out with accounts published and written by outsiders as well.

3. *When was the text written?* More recent works are likely to provide you with more accurate information on historical subjects, simply because they can take account of all the material that has been written. On the other hand, sometimes you will want to examine older accounts to determine the way certain subjects were dealt with at the time. For example, if you are studying Mormon views towards blacks, it makes a great difference whether the article was written before or after the Mormon hierarchy altered its views. You might try to locate sources from both periods, in order to compare their interpretations.

Be sure to write down the date of publication for each source you use, so you can sit down later and look at them in chronological order. Note that the copyright date on a book might be quite misleading, since the original version of the book may have been published much earlier. The card catalogue or the preface or introduction to the book will often tell you the original date of publication, which is important. At the same time, if you are dealing with a book that is a second or third edition, note both the original date and the date of this edition, and read the preface or introduction to determine if very significant changes were made.

4. *What is the tone or style of the text?* Is the author attempting to persuade the reader that the religion is true, or that the reader should join? Or is the writer attempting to be somewhat "dispassionate," reviewing information or opinions? Once again, either tone may be useful or appropriate, but you want to try to use sources with varying styles.

5. *How do the source's facts and opinions fit with other sources you have read?* As you read several pieces, you may begin to note disagreements between your sources. Although this is confusing, it is also the most worthwhile part of doing research, because it will force you to go back and ask two questions: (a) Why is there this disagreement? and (b) What does the disagreement mean?

You will need to distinguish here between disagreements about facts and disagreements about opinions. Factual disagreements might merely reflect differing amounts of knowledge about what happened. But they might also be caused by underlying faith or value commitments; it is usually difficult for people who believe strongly in anything to acknowledge facts that undercut their views. Your task is to try to uncover these sources of disagreement. Your paper will be much richer if you can present some of the conflicting viewpoints you have found and try to account for the differences. In many cases, you will not be able to determine which position is "correct," and there is no reason why you have to do so. What is more important is that you learn to see your sources, not as absolute beacons of truth, but as examples of people and communities trying to understand and explain the world as they see it.

You may find it harder to adopt this perspective when you are reading secondary sources (such as historical accounts) than when you are reading the primary faith statements of a community. But it is important to keep your eyes open to all of these questions when reading any book or article, even something that appears to be wholly objective and purely descriptive. Remember that you are the key interpreter in your paper, and that your sources are data that you can rely on only to the extent that *you* decide they are trustworthy. That is a difficult judgment to make, but it is a necessary one if your paper is going to be more than a summary of what other people have said.

In choosing your sources in the library, try to achieve a balance between different sorts of texts. In your initial search, include some primary and some secondary sources, some written by insiders and some by outsiders, some historical accounts and some more polemical discussions or arguments. Of course, what you need to examine will depend upon your topic, but a good general rule to follow is that your paper will be more balanced, trustworthy, and convincing the more diverse the sources you have used.

TAKING NOTES

When you read a book or an article, listen to a lecture, or interview an expert, the information will be recorded in your mind but may not remain there very long. No one has perfect recall, and the more information you gather, the more difficult it will be to remember precisely what it was and where you found it. For these reasons, taking notes is one of the most crucial aspects of writing a research paper.

Whether you decide to use index cards, sheets of paper, or a computer terminal, certain basic rules apply to note taking:

1. Your notes are designed to allow *you* to use them later. Notes do not have to be legible to anyone other than you; they do not have to—and, indeed, should not—answer questions other people might be interested in asking. Use whatever abbreviations, forms of expression, or shorthand you are comfortable with.

2. Notes must allow you to reconstruct both what was said and who said it. If you carelessly summarize a point made by a writer, you might have to go back later and check precisely what was said about a related point. In addition, you are expected to be able to account for everything you write in a paper, if it is not your own idea. Therefore, always accurately represent in your notes what was said in the source, and document where you found it.

3. Notes should be extensive enough to answer your research questions, but short enough to be manageable and useful in constructing your paper. If you read ten five-page articles and take five-pages of notes on each article, you might as well simply copy the articles. The point of notes is to *extract selectively* the key points that deal with your themes and issues. If you err on the side of taking too few notes, you will find yourself unable to write a fully documented and thoroughly researched paper. If you err on the side of taking too many notes, you will spend countless hours sorting through thoroughly irrelevant amounts of data to get to the few points you want to include in your paper.

This is probably the hardest thing to learn about taking notes, and there are no easy ways to learn it except to simply start doing it and check what you have done periodically. For example, after reading the first three or four sources, look back over your notes and ask yourself whether you need all the information you have included, or whether there are other pieces of information you wish you had included.

4. Separate out important information. You can do this in several ways, such as by underlining key phrases or points, indenting key themes or passages in your notes, or keeping a separate list (referenced to each card or page of your notes) of these more important points.

Before you begin to take notes, read over the section on footnotes and bibliography in this book (Chapter 13), so you will know the proper form of citation to use. This will save you an enormous amount of time later on. Your notes (whether on index cards, paper, or computer) should include all the information you will need in writing your final draft, so be sure to take down all the relevant information.

You can take notes on index cards, on 8 1/2 × 11-inch paper, or a computer terminal if you have one available to you. In any event, you should be sure to write down all the bibliographic information about the reference on your notes. For books, include the following:

BIBLIOGRAPHIC INFORMATION ON BOOKS

Author's complete name

Title (including any subtitle that might appear after a colon in the title at the beginning of the book)

Translator (if there is one, the name will be listed on the title page of the book)

Place of publication (e.g., Englewood Cliffs, N.J.; or New York)

Publisher's name (e.g., Prentice Hall)

Date of publication (include original date of publication if your copy is listed as a later edition [second, third, etc.], or if the book is translated)

For articles, include the following information in your notes:

BIBLIOGRAPHIC INFORMATION ON ARTICLES

Author's complete name

Title

Name of periodical or volume in which article appears

Volume number

Date of journal or volume

Pages on which article appears

If the article appears in a book of collected articles, write down all the information about the book (as listed above) as well as about the article, because you will need to list this information in your footnotes or bibliography.

Some people keep separate bibliographic entry cards, using one for each source consulted; others prefer to write the full bibliographic information on the top of the first card used for each source. It doesn't matter which system you use, so long as you always remember to keep track of all the information and where you gathered it from.

If you are using separate bibligraphy cards, your source cards will look like the following. If you are not using separate cards to list the sources, the same information is simply written out at the top of the first card or note page.

Jones, Alfred
How I Keep Up with the Smiths
Chicago, Illinois
Status Publishing Co.
1988

Jones, Alfred, and Jones, Mildred
"Why We Can't Keep Up with the Smiths"
Journal of Status Studies
Volume 100
September 30, 1988
pp. 20–26

Smith, Susan

"Why the Jones Family Can't Keep Up with Us" in Franklin, Benjamin (editor)

Those Amazing Smith and Jones Families

Philadelphia

Status Publishing Co.

1988

pp. 100–121

Write down the page number where each particular point you have written appears, in case you need to footnote that point or quotation in your paper. Gathering information in this way will save you a lot of time later on.

If you are using index cards, it is preferable to limit yourself to one idea (or quotation) from each source on a card. This will help you organize your notes later, because you can simply sort the various cards by topic. If you are taking notes on paper or computer, you can do the same thing, either by using one page for each topic or by putting a "new page" code after each topic on your computer. Again, the method is up to you, but the important thing is to be clear and consistent.

Your notes should be legible and complete. Write in pen wherever possible, and use abbreviations of your own only when you are sure you will remember what the abbreviation stands for. Write on only one side of your cards or paper. Be sure to put all direct quotations from your source in quotation marks, and note any quotations within quotations with single apostrophes. For example: " 'The pacifism of the early Christians was more a function of necessity than belief,' according to one writer" (p. 24).

In this example, note that the entire passage is in quotation marks because it is a verbatim quote from the source; the section enclosed in apostrophes is a quotation found in the source itself. The page number at the end of the citation is your notation of where this passage is found in your source. (If the writer is someone you might want to track down later, be sure to make an additional note about the reference, including the page number where that quote came from.)

If you find some particularly interesting and well-stated passages, you should write them down as they appear, being sure to put them in quotation marks to remind yourself that these are the author's words, not your own. Paraphrase other sections, summarizing the main points for future reference.

When you read an article at the early stages of your research, be sure to look carefully at the bibliography (or footnotes or end notes, if there is no bibliography) for lists of other articles or books that might be interesting. Sometimes an article will not generate any material directly for your use but will provide you with extremely important references for future use. Remember to write down the complete citation of each article, and keep a separate list of all such articles.

Keep your notes in a safe place. It is useful to begin organizing them by subject as soon as possible, since this will allow you to notice which topics you need to continue to research. For example, if you are studying the views of Muslims toward women's equality, you might be looking for information about the history of Islam's attitudes toward women, current opinion on the subject, and the underlying justifications for the various positions. If you keep your notes separate on these different areas of your topic, you might recognize that you have a lot of information already on the second two topics but very little on the history. This would remind you to devote more time researching the first area of your topic.

CONCLUDING COMMENTS

Remember that your notes are designed to help you write your paper. They are not meant to impress anyone about how much research you have done, nor will they help you make sense of the information unless you have organized them appropriately. Therefore, it is a good idea to spend some time figuring out the system with which you are most comfortable, and taking care to develop a set of notes that are concise, well documented, clear, and focused on the subject you will write about in your paper.

6

Field Research: Philosophical and Methodological Issues

As a field researcher, your primary task is to *understand* what you are studying. You are not trying to discover the meaning of life, or to make friends, or to work through your own doubts and uncertainties about the truth of religious claims. Your job is to figure out what is happening and to communicate what you have discovered in a clear and interesting manner. The purpose of this chapter is to identify some assumptions and principles of research that specifically apply to doing field research.

ASSUMPTIONS OF FIELD RESEARCH

All field research involves three essential assumptions. First, there must be an object to be studied, something we term "reality" or "the way things are." If we do not believe that there is something out there that is independent of us, then there is no point in beginning the examination. In this situation, the object of study is a religious organization or tradition, with a complex set of features (such as beliefs and rituals) that exist, and have existed, independently of any research that may have been conducted.

Second, we believe that it is possible to gather information about that reality. We refer to that information as *data,* a word meaning something that is "given." The assumption is that the researcher, by careful investigation, can find information that provides knowledge about the object. For example, by watching a worship service, you can gather data about how people pray, and that information answers questions that led you to conduct the research in the first place.

Third, the researcher assumes that what is being studied can be ordered, made sense of, organized. There would be no point in conducting research if we believed that we were studying something that was completely random and arbitrary. After all, what could we say about such a reality? The goal of understanding, of explaining, is reasonable only if we believe that the world we know can be understood and explained.

If we take these assumptions seriously, then good researchers will respect the reality that is studied, will work hard and systematically to gather data about it, and will seek to order that data in as helpful and as thorough a way as possible.

PROBLEMS OF SOCIAL RESEARCH

To make sure that your research accomplishes its goals, you must raise several issues before beginning a project. These issues are fundamental, and they are questions that should "bother" you throughout your research. Although each issue raises highly complicated philosophical and scientific problems, we will merely present them briefly to sensitize you to their importance.

Validity

If our task is to understood something about the world, we must be concerned about trying to assure that we are in fact reflecting that world rather than something else. We speak about the "validity" of research in the same way we would talk about the validity of a driver's license. Your license is valid if it is authentic, up to date, and stamped by the appropriate authorities. Similarly, a result (often called a finding) of a research project is valid if it authentically expresses something about the current nature of the object under study. Asking about validity reminds us to worry about whether our research is really picking up on what is "out there," rather than spinning off imaginary results. Most of our suggestions throughout this section are designed to help you produce a piece of valid research.

The most likely source of invalid results stems from our inability to draw appropriate conclusions from what we have found. A result might be invalid if it claims to have proven much more than can be reasonably inferred from the research itself. For example, if you have attended two services at a Buddhist temple, you are unlikely to be able to make general statements about what Buddhists believe or how Buddhists pray, without making it very clear that your conclusions are limited to a very small number of observations. We want our conclusions as well as our methods to be trustworthy and solid, accurately reflecting the world as it is.

Reliability

A second question often asked of research projects is whether they are reliable. The term *reliability* means the same as it does in our everyday life. What would it mean to call a friend "reliable"? It would mean that you could count on him, that he would be there tomorrow just as he is today. A reliable research finding is one that can also be counted on not to change from day to day.

Even though you are conducting a single study in one organization, you should be concerned about reliability as well. One way to do so is to ask yourself: "Could someone else, coming into this same organization, discover what I have discovered?" If your answer is no, then you need to rethink whether you can count on your data. For example, if you are gathering your information in a way that leads people to give you purely arbitrary answers to questions, then you (or anyone else) might get the opposite answer from those people tomorrow. The best way to guard against problems of reliability is to be systematic and careful in conducting your research.

Research is reliable only if the researcher provides sufficient information about how the information was gathered to enable anyone else to repeat the research and draw similar conclusions. Of course, if you are attending a service, no one else will ever have the opportunity to attend that same service in the future. But you can explain your procedures and analysis carefully enough to convince someone else that, had they been there, they would have drawn the same conclusions, and therefore your research and conclusions will be seen as reliable.

Note that both validity and reliability are based upon honesty and trust in both the content and the methods of the research. The key difference (and the reason why both are so necessary) is that validity involves the ability to accurately describe the object of study, while reliability concerns the extent to which our methods could lead someone else to the same conclusions. We judge research findings by both standards, in order to make sure that our attention is focused both on the accuracy of our results and the care with which we have proceeded in our data gathering.

Objectivity

Related to both validity and reliability issues is another problem of conducting research: namely, the difficulty of being objective. Since the assumption is that there is an independent reality to be discovered, any biases or feelings of the researcher might prevent us from seeing "the world as it really is." If the goal is to understand and explain something (such as the ritual life of a congregation), our own prejudices are likely to hinder us from providing a completely accurate account.

Debates about the objectivity of research are complicated. But the basic insight you should have in beginning your research is to recognize that, while maintaining objectivity is extremely important and valuable, complete objectivity is impossible, and perhaps not even desirable. Part of the problem is that the very notion of "being objective" means many different things, only some of which are essential for a researcher.

For the sake of clarifying the point, think for a moment about the following situation. You and several classmates are sitting around a table, in the middle of which is a large cube. The cube has different colors on each side, and only one side is visible to each of you. Your task is to describe the cube. Can you do so objectively?

Using this example, we see that there are certain important ways in which you can (and should) be objective. You should be willing to report what color the cube looks like from your vantage point, and to do so regardless of what your own favorite color is (or whether you made a bet with someone else before you sat down that you would see a blue cube on the table). You should also be open to the way the cube looks to other people; if a fellow student sees a different color, this is more "data" that you need to think about before insisting on your own answer. And you need to look carefully and systematically at the cube, rather than just glancing at it out of the corner of your eye.

We have just identified three fundamental standards of objective research in this discussion: honesty, open-mindedness, and systematic examination. A good researcher is honest about what is seen and strives to avoid being blinded by biases, prejudices, or wishes. A good researcher is open-minded, willing to consider alternative explanations and take other people's research into account. And a good researcher is systematic, using whatever tools are available in a thorough manner to do the best possible job of understanding what is being studied. These are ways in which we can and must be objective.

AN OBJECTIVE RESEARCHER IS

Honest

Open-minded

Systematic

However, there are some ways in which we are going to be limited by the fact that *we* are conducting the research. Much of this limitation simply comes with the territory of being human—namely, we are finite creatures. I am able to sit in only one chair at a time. I can use only the senses I have, and some of them might not be perfectly functioning (for example, if I am color-blind, I will not report seeing the cube "accurately"). I may have had bad experiences with similar experiments before and find it difficult to participate in such studies.

The point is a rather simple one: We always observe and learn selectively, through the subjective lenses we have as finite and imperfect creatures. But that fact does not mean we can give up on seeking to be objective. In addition to following the three standards suggested above (honesty, open-mindedness, and systematic exploration), we can try to apply these standards to the very problem of our subjectivity. We can be honest about what our biases are, and in so doing try to make sure that they color our research to the smallest possible extent. We can be willing to hear other people's perspectives and use them to question our own perspective and limitations. And we can seek to view things from different angles, not in the hope of eliminating our own point of view, but as a means of checking our all-too-human tendency to equate *our* view with *the* view.

In short, we urge you to be as self-aware as possible about the situations in which you find it hard, or impossible, to be objective. If you are turned off or disgusted by something that happens during your research, don't feel guilty about the feeling. Instead, admit it, think about it, and *use* it as a piece of data in your research. If you cannot appreciate someone's statement of belief because it conflicts with your own, recognize this fact, and try to figure out where the disagreement lies and why it is so important to you.

If you remind yourself periodically about the difficulties of conducting research that is valid, reliable, and objective, you will become a more self-aware and conscientious researcher, and the process and results of your work will reflect those values.

SOME GUIDELINES FOR PARTICIPANT OBSERVATION

The somewhat abstract points we have made so far have major implications for how you proceed as you begin your empirical research. In studying a religious organization, you will be functioning primarily as a "participant observer," a fancy phrase that simply means that, while you are taking part in some activities of the group you are studying, you are there to observe and understand what is happening. In this section, we will suggest some broad "rules" to follow in adopting that role. Pay close attention to these basic guidelines, because they determine everything you will do in your research.

1. You Are a Participant and an Observer, but Not a Member.

This is a crucial distinction to bear in mind throughout your research project. Indeed, it is so important that the very choice of your research subject is dependent upon it. *Do not study a group to which you already belong, nor should you join the group in order to conduct your research.* Members identify themselves as belonging to organizations; they may pay dues, attend meetings regularly, help determine policy, or just be willing to answer a question by saying, "I am a member of X." A member has an investment in the group.

As a researcher, you do not belong to the group you are studying. You may indeed participate in some of its activities, such as attending religious services or group meetings; but you are doing so *only* to understand how the group functions and what it would feel like to be a member. The researcher remains an "outsider" even when taking part in group activities.

2. Observe and Ask Questions as an Outsider, Not as an Insider.

Because you are not a member, you have a unique ability to adopt a different perspective. This is why it is so important to remain an outsider. You do not have any personal stake in whether the group survives or crumbles, gains or loses members, is correct or incorrect in its doctrine or practice. As a result, you are able to stand back and try to see the way the group functions, without being influenced by the needs or interests of its members.

This is not an easy task. Indeed, it may be the hardest part of conducting social research. You will have to train yourself to be objective, to ask questions from a more neutral standpoint, to avoid becoming influenced by the way the situation may look to the members themselves. All researchers have this difficulty; it is something that must be learned and relearned every time you begin a project, and something to keep reminding yourself of throughout the project.

3. Understanding Depends upon Imagination.

This is a difficult concept to grasp, but it is fundamental to the stance of the social researcher. Although you must strive to maintain your role as an outsider, you cannot simply pretend that you are a robot or an automaton processing information. You are being asked to study a group composed of human beings, and you need to understand what the *experience* of membership is for these people.

The term *understand* itself suggests the importance of this requirement. You need to imagine yourself in the place of the members, and ask yourself questions such as, "What does this feel like to them? What needs of theirs are being met? Why would they keep coming back to these meetings?"

There is a fine balance here between becoming so "understanding" that you forget that you are an outsider, and standing so far apart that you cannot gain any feel for the group or its members. Again, that is something you will have to struggle with as you conduct your research. Remember that it is a problem that all researchers face, so don't become discouraged at the difficulty of the task.

4. Your Identity as a Researcher Should Be Open.

You do not need to wear a sign announcing that you are attending a service only because you are enrolled in a course, nor do you need to tell everyone you meet that you are "merely a researcher." But you should respect the group's right to know who you are, why you are there, and how you are going to use what they tell you. The rules are simple rules of both etiquette and ethics, and common sense and honesty should serve you well.

For example, you should identify yourself as a student doing research whenever you approach anyone for an interview, or when you first call and ask about attending services or meetings. In addition, if anyone asks you who you are or what you are doing there, tell them briefly about the project and why you are studying their group. (A simple "I have been interested in this [religious group] for a while, and wanted to learn more about it" will suffice.) When in doubt, answer briefly and honestly.

However, you do not have to feel that you are being made the object of someone else's research or questioning. If people ask you questions about your own religious beliefs, memberships, or feelings, try to deflect the questions by reminding them that you are there to study *their* group. If you wish, you might want to offer to discuss your own views with them at a later time.

5. Observe, Observe, Observe.

As a researcher, you have several tools that you have carried around with you all your life: your mind and your senses. You have always used them, but now you will have to be more aware of disciplining them.

The key to productive research is to be sensitive with all aspects of one's being: Keep your eyes open, listen carefully, and think slowly and carefully about what is being said. Pay attention not only to what is happening externally, but what is happening inside you as well. For example, are you feeling uncomfortable, embarrassed, uneasy, aroused, moved, bored?

Once again, you will find that it is not an easy task to observe in this manner. You will have to learn when to pay more attention to external events and when to focus on your own reactions, when to attend to seeing, and when to listen. You will learn to become more sensitive, and to be able to listen and look more effectively, the more often you observe.

This is why you should try to do as many different observational activities as possible. Try to attend several religious services, instead of just one or two; if possible, go to some other meetings of the group's committees or activities. Talk not just to the main clergyperson, but to some other staff and members. Try to go to the group's sanctuary when it is empty, and show up early enough to see people arriving. The more situations you can place yourself in, the richer your observations will be, and the more practiced an observer you will become.

6. Remember That, as a Participant Observer, You Have a Right to Be There.

Religious institutions in the United States are almost always extremely open to people attending their services. Most groups welcome newcomers, and people will usually be interested in your research and your interest in them. Don't feel embarrassed or dishonest about being there, and don't feel (or act!) like a spy.

It is perfectly natural to be nervous and anxious about conducting field research. After all, you are walking into a strange situation, where unexpected things can happen. If you avoid beginning your research because of these fears, talk about them with a friend or with your instructor. Remember, however, that everyone is somewhat uncomfortable with new situations and strangers, but that the process becomes much easier as you continue.

You may stumble across a group that prefers not to have outsiders present. You can minimize the chance of embarrassment by making a phone call to the group before you plan to attend your first meeting. If, by some chance, you are asked to leave by an usher or other group official, do so. If possible, however, ask them why you are being excluded, and whether you can come back at another time to speak to someone in the group about their activities and beliefs. If they decline, choose another group for your research.

Such occurrences are extemely unlikely. Indeed, it is far more probable that you will be besieged with questions and offers to stay for coffee or to participate in other activities. Within the boundaries set by our earlier guidelines, take full advantage of the opportunities for more detailed observation provided by such offers.

As you begin planning and conducting your research, continue to think about the various issues we have raised in this chapter. How can you ensure that your research is valid and reliable? How can you maintain sufficient objectivity without sacrificing understanding? What methods are most useful in maintaining your status as a participant observer?

7

Elements of Participant Observation: An Overview

Within the guidelines discussed in earlier chapters, how should you conduct your field research? In this chapter, we will provide an overview, including some hints about developing themes and questions, choosing the group, entering the setting, observing, and describing and analyzing the research group.

In later chapters, we will return in more detail to issues related to asking questions, interviewing, and analyzing your data. We strongly recommend, therefore, that you read through the entire book before beginning your field work. But this chapter will provide you with a good indication of how to proceed.

You should read (or reread) the sections of this book dealing with assumptions related to participant observation (Chapter 6) and selecting a topic (Chapter 3). All of the points made in those sections are relevant for your empirical research and should be done *before* you begin your observations. However, you might want to attend a service or two to help define your subject.

CHOOSING THE RESEARCH GROUP

Your instructor may provide you with some guidance concerning the group or groups to be studied. Follow those instructions carefully. You can find information about different groups in local newspapers (which list religious services, times, and places), the telephone book, or by a walking or driving tour of the area. In addition to your instructor's guidance, there are three major criteria for choosing a group:

1. Do not choose a group to which you already belong. The only exception that might be made is if your particular religious tradition forbids you from attending any other religion's services. If this is the case, discuss the matter with your instructor before deciding to study your own religious group.

2. Choose a group you are interested in learning about. The basis for this interest could be that you once attended a service with a friend, or that one of your present friends is a member, or that you read something about the group that intrigued you, or some other reason. The reason is less important than that you have one. The research will be much more challenging and enjoyable if you study something you want to learn about.

3. Choose a group that is accessible to you and has enough activities and meetings for you to study in the time available to you. If your first choice is a group that is so far away that you will be able to attend only two meetings or conduct two interviews, you are better off studying a second or third choice that is closer and more convenient. If the group has its religious services at a time you cannot attend, find another one to study. You may need to make a series of phone calls to determine which group is most appropriate for you.

ENTERING THE RESEARCH SETTING

Once you have tentatively chosen the group, decide upon a strategy for beginning the research. In most cases, this will involve three related steps:

1. determining the time and place of religious services,

2. attending at least one such service, and

3. speaking with someone in the group about getting more information.

It is easy to find out where and when services are held. Most newspapers will list this information (see the "Religion" section of the Saturday edition of your local newspaper), and telephone books routinely list the groups as well (check in the Yellow Pages under "Religious Organizations"). We recommend that you make a telephone call during the week before you are planning on attending the service. Simply inform the person who answers the phone that you are a student who would like to attend a service, and ask where and when the services are held. Making this call can save you time and might also provide you with some information about the religious group. (*Your research begins as soon as you dial the phone.* Make some brief notes to yourself about the conversation with the switchboard operator, even if that is all the contact you have had so far.)

Many religious organizations have more than one service on their day of worship. If possible, try to attend the largest or "main" service of the day. If in doubt, ask the person on the phone which service has the greatest attendance. In most Christian churches, there is a service around 11 o'clock that is usually the main service. In Jewish services, either Friday night or Saturday morning is the main service (as a general rule, Reform stresses Friday night, and Conservative and Orthodox Saturday morning, although this is not always the case). In Islam, the main service is held on Friday. Other religions may hold services at different times, so a phone call is the best way to find out.

Once you decide which service to attend, carefully prepare yourself for your first major observation. The following preobservation steps are highly recommended.

THINGS TO DO BEFORE YOUR FIRST VISIT

I.   Write down some themes you are interested in exploring for your paper. (Read Chapter 3 for suggestions.)

II. Make a list of key points to observe in the service, and how you intend to focus on them. (Example: "Look for use of music in the service and how it seems to affect people. Attend to the expressions on people's faces, body movements, and so on.")

III. If available, read some brief background information on the religious organization of which your particular group is a part. (Refer to the information in Appendix 1, as well as any relevant readings in your other course texts.)

IV. Make a list of your expectations, fears, and concerns about attending the service. This provides you with an excellent opportunity to recognize any preconceptions or biases you may be bringing with you into the research. In making your list, try to answer the following questions:

1. What impressions do you have about the religious tradition itself? Have you heard negative things about it or its members? Do you have any stereotypes about people who are members of this religion?

2. What do you think the service will be like? What type of people do you think you will find there? How do you think they will act? What sort of atmosphere do you expect?

3. How do you think you will be treated? Do you expect to feel welcomed or ignored? Are you afraid of being embarrassed and singled out? Are you nervous about not knowing anyone, and about not knowing how to act?

4. Where do you think your preconceptions come from? Can you trace them to any earlier experiences, to reading, or to any other source?

V. Consider asking someone else to attend the first service with you. This person might be a member of the group, but preferably should not be. Discuss with that person what you will be looking for.

On the day of the service, be sure to dress appropriately. You might want to ask about attire when you make your phone call to the religious group. In most cases, however, just dress neatly and modestly (no jeans, shorts, or loud colors). Don't feel that you have to get extremely dressed up, however; it is important that you feel comfortable with what you wear.

Certain religious traditions may place more stringent requirements on worshippers. For example, Muslims expect women to avoid exposing any part of the body (including the hair) at worship services; in addition, people with any bleeding (including women who are menstruating) are not allowed to attend Islamic services, and certain washings may be required before entering. Again, a phone call is the best way to avoid embarrassment or being prevented from attending.

Leave enough time to arrive at the service at least fifteen minutes before it is scheduled to begin. When you arrive, spend a few minutes outside the building looking at the neighborhood, the type of building, and any interesting architectural features (including religious symbols on the outside).

When you go in, follow the instructions (if any) provided by the ushers. If there is no such guidance, find a seat in a part of the room that allows you maximum observation range. You will probably be most comfortable sitting toward the back, which also allows you to follow cues from the members as the service proceeds.

Sit quietly and attentively, watching and listening as people enter.

SITTING THROUGH A SERVICE

Religious services vary enormously. The key to observing a service is to get a feel for the flow of what is happening, and to observe as carefully as possible how people are responding at each stage of the service. If a program is provided, quickly read through it before the service begins, but most of your attention should be directed toward the building and the people who are coming in.

During the service, follow the basic cues provided by other people in the congregation. Unless you feel uncomfortable doing so, participate in the service: Stand when the congregation stands, sing the songs, read responses along with the members. If you prefer, you can sit or stand silently at such moments.

There are certain parts of the service in which it may be inappropriate for you to participate, and some of this might have to be learned by trial and error. For example, in most Christian services, only baptized Christians are expected to participate in the Eucharist (the eating of the bread and the drinking of the wine); in Roman Catholic services, only baptized Roman Catholics should take part in communion. If you are not baptized, just sit silently during this part of the service, observing what people are doing and how they seem to be affected by the experience. If you are baptized, you may choose to take part in the Eucharist, but you might also decide to sit back and observe.

In other cases, there may be activities in which you are unable or unwilling to participate. For example, a Muslim service might have prayer techniques that are athletically too demanding, and Buddhist or Hindu temples might require you to sit in an uncomfortable position for a long period of time. If you are physically unable to participate, or if your own religious views prevent you from doing some of these activities, just sit or stand quietly and observe for a while. Otherwise, we suggest that you try to participate, at least long enough to get a sense of what the activity might feel like.

Chapter 8 outlines some specific elements of the service to look for. In general, try to be as open as you can to what is going on. Look and listen not just for what is on your list, but for unexpected events and feelings. Look around at various parts of the congregation occasionally, rather than always focusing your attention on the front of the room. In periods of group silence, attend to what people are doing.

If possible, jot down some brief notes during the service, to jog your memory later on. You might use the program provided, or a small piece of paper in your pocket. Do not try to take extensive notes, however, since that will just distract you (and those around you). In some situations, writing during the service is not allowed (such as in Orthodox or many Conservative Jewish services, and in Muslim services); if you are in doubt, you might ask the usher when you first arrive about their policy. If someone asks you to stop writing during the service, just put the paper away and try to take mental notes.

If you are at a service that consists primarily of silent meditation (such as a Friends meeting or a Buddhist service), you will not be able to take notes. At such a service, there are two important kinds of observation that you should perform, however. First, observe how the other people are behaving. Are they sitting? Are their eyes closed? Do they seem to be praying to themselves? Is the silence ever interrupted by any activity or sounds?

In addition, part of your task at such a service should be to try to experience the silence yourself. If you can read something beforehand about the religion's understanding of the meaning of silence or meditation, do so. In most cases, the key is to clear one's mind of extraneous thoughts, and try to allow the silence to place one in closer contact to the sacred (however that might be expressed by the particular religious tradition). You should try this as well. If you have never sat silently and meditated, this will be a strange and difficult experience, but it is an important part of your observation and will give you some useful information about the practice.

When the service ends, sit and watch people as they leave, continuing your observation.

AFTER THE SERVICE

Try to allow enough time after the service to speak with some members of the group. You might attend the informal gathering that often occurs immediately following the service. If no one comes up to you and asks you who you are, find someone who is alone and introduce yourself, saying you would like to talk to them about the group. We know it is hard to just walk up to a stranger in such a situation, but almost everyone will be very responsive and willing to talk. If they are not, just continue to watch and observe what is happening.

If the person who led the service is present, try to talk to her or him after the service. Introduce yourself, and ask whether you can make an appointment to ask some further questions. (See Chapter 9 on interviewing.) If there are other people who seem interested, ask them about setting up a time to talk further as well. Use your first time in the setting as an opportunity to build some contacts and opportunities for your research.

Finally, before leaving, try to get some written literature about the religious organization. Ask an usher or another member whether they have any brochures or informational material giving historical or descriptive data about the group. If they have a library, ask when it is open and whether you could come back to look through their materials.

DESCRIBING YOUR OBSERVATIONS

As soon as you leave the building, this round of observation ends, but your work does not. As soon as possible (preferably immediately), take out a piece of paper and jot down as many notes as you can about what you observed. Include everything you can remember, however insignificant it might appear to be: number of people present, type and color of clothing, sounds and smells, impressions and feelings (again, refer to Chapter 8 for some suggestions). Just write down enough to jog your memory later when you can write more detailed notes.

Within the next few hours, sit down in a quiet place and, using the brief notes you have already written, write out an extended description of your observation. Begin by indicating the date, place, and time of the observation, the nature of the observation (religious service, meeting, etc.), whether you were alone, and when you are writing the description. Include as much detail as possible in your elaborated notes.

Try to distinguish between things you saw or feelings you had at the time of the service, and your current feelings and thoughts in looking back on it now. (You might want to put the latter comments in brackets, or use a different color of ink or type to set them off.) *Be thorough.* After the first twenty-four hours, you can count on remembering very little of what you observed. (Appendix 3 provides some examples of what your field notes should look like.)

In addition, read over the notes you wrote before the service about your expectations and fears. Write down (in a "before–after" format) what the experience was actually like. For example:

1. Were your expectations met? Was the experience easier or more difficult than you had imagined?

2. Did anything surprise you? Did anything happen that you had never seen (or even heard of) before?

3. How did the service compare to other religious services you have attended? What were the major similarities and differences?

Chapter 10 ("Analyzing the Data") provides more detailed suggestions on how to organize and use your notes.

THE RANGE OF OBSERVATIONAL OPPORTUNITIES

We have discussed your entry into the setting in terms of a religious service. But there are numerous other types of observations you might make, depending upon the nature and scope of the research project. We recommend attending a service first, in order to orient yourself to the central ritual of the group. In some cases, you might have to conduct an interview or attend a meeting before going to a service, however.

Try to set up as many different types of observations as possible, and organize them in a coherent fashion. We believe the following is an optimal (although not the only acceptable) order for conducting your field research.

AN IDEAL SCHEDULE FOR YOUR RESEARCH

1. Make a telephone contact with the group
2. Read some material about the group
3. Attend a service
4. Read some more material about the group (including literature they might give to you)
5. Attend another service
6. Interview clergyperson or group leader
7. Interview a staff person or member
8. Attend another group function (or two or three!)
9. Interview other members
10. Attend additional services or meetings

[*Note:* Not included in this outline are the various steps related to note-taking, transcribing interviews, outlining your paper, etc.]

Although there is nothing sacred about this schedule, it will allow you to approach each event with sufficient background and openness to get the most out of each experience. For example, if you interview the group leader before you have attended a service or two, you are less likely to know the key questions you need to ask that person about the group's theology or symbols. Similarly, if you interview group members before you have attended some other function, you will not be able to ask them about their own participation and views of the different activities.

How much you do depends on both the nature of your topic and the expectations your instructor has created for the project. What is more important is that you think carefully about the order and structure of your various observations, in order that they provide you with as much new knowledge as possible. As you move from observation to observation, think about whether there are other people you need to talk to, or other events you need to attend. For instance, you might find that you want to attend a service at a different time (or on a different day), to determine whether the people attending that service have different experiences or characteristics.

CONCLUDING COMMENTS

Behind these guidelines and suggestions stands the central insight with which we began: Your task is to understand what the religious group is like.

Your stance in doing so is as a participant observer, requiring you to enter the world you are studying and to imaginatively recreate for yourself the experience of the members, but to do so always as an outsider. Your tools are your senses and your mind, and your skills as an observer are measured by your ability to attend not only to what you see, hear, feel, and experience in the religious setting but also to attend to your own inner states and reactions to the situation.

8
What to Look For

You are sitting in a religious service, watching people you don't know repeating odd phrases and performing strange rituals. Or you speak with a friend about her religious beliefs and find that the language she uses is filled with unusual concepts and unintelligible phrases. Or you are talking with a group of classmates, and you suddenly discover that you are the only person in the group who was brought up with different religious values and principles. You may find yourself confused in such situations, wondering what is happening, why it seems so strange to you, and how it could make so much sense to those who are taking part.

In this chapter, we will suggest what to look at in your quest to understand the religious group you are examining. You will not be able to examine all (or even most) of these factors in your project, simply because of time and energy limitations. What you choose to focus on should be determined both by your own interests and by the nature of the particular organization you have chosen.

For the purposes of simplifying the discussion, we will divide religious experience into three categories.[1] Although religion is a highly complex phe-

---

[1] These categories are based on the work of sociologist Joachim Wach, particularly in his book *Sociology of Religion* (University of Chicago Press, 1944).

nomenon that is hard to separate out into different components, it is helpful to identify three different ways in which religion manifests itself, and in which people experience and live out their religious identities.

THREE EXPRESSIONS OF RELIGION

1. **Belief** (the theoretical dimension)

2. **Ritual** (the practical dimension)

3. **Community** (the social dimension)

The first category is that of religious **belief**. Belief is an act both of the mind and of the heart; we believe what we assume or want to be true but are unable to prove or see directly. (If we could prove or see it, it would be known rather than believed.) Religious belief is the realm of assertions, statements, and feelings one may have about any religious object, such as God, one's religious community, the Bible, or salvation. Beliefs are at once individual and shared, and religious communities are defined in part by a set of common beliefs held by persons who identify themselves with that particular faith community.

We have two ways to determine what people believe. Most obviously, we can ask them what they believe: "Do you believe in God?" "What do you believe happens when people die?" "Do you believe the Koran is completely true in everything it says?" "What is the nature of evil and suffering?" Sometimes people will tell you what they believe even if you don't ask; for example, sermons are usually designed to tell the congregation what the preacher believes, whether or not the people have asked for such an answer.

But we can also learn about beliefs indirectly, by drawing conclusions on the basis of how people act and what they are doing. If someone acts in a highly respectful manner around a particular object, for example, we may assume that, in some sense, he or she believes that object to be holy or sacred. Precisely because we can often draw such conclusions about belief on the basis of action, our categories are not airtight. The second element of religion is the realm of religious action or ritual.

For our purposes, religious **ritual** consists of what people do when they are acting together as a religious community in worship, reflection, or study. Ritual is something external, visible, readily apparent to the observer. In an interesting way, ritual both results from and creates belief. You have probably had the experience of finding that you enjoyed doing something the more you did it, even though you were dubious about it at the start. Such experiences are analogous to how belief is strengthened and recreated in religious communities, and it is for that reason that ritual is important in its own right, and not merely a substitute for, or a more superficial version of, belief.

Finally, religious belief and ritual are usually collective enterprises, enacted in **community**. The community aspect of religious experience directs our attention toward the way in which a group of people gather together for religious purposes. Of course, there is no religious community without belief and ritual; but, at the same time, there is no sustained belief or ritual without an ongoing community to pass on the beliefs and to share in enacting the rituals.

An example of the community aspect of a religious group is the question of the characteristics of the members. Who are these people who are believing these beliefs and enacting these rituals? Where are they from, how old are they, what do they do for a living? If we looked only at the beliefs or the rituals, we would not attend to the equally important fact that religious groups (like all groups) need to find people to share those beliefs and rituals if they are to survive.

The remainder of this chapter consists of some suggested issues to focus on within each of these three categories. Remember, however, that these three elements of religious experience are highly connected and dependent upon each other. In distinguishing between them, we do not want to leave the impression that one can have belief without ritual or community, or that ritual could exist without a supporting structure of belief and a continuing community, or that community would have any meaning without a shared set of beliefs and rituals. Only in recognizing the fascinating connections between these elements can we begin to appreciate the richness and complexity of religious experience.

RELIGIOUS BELIEF

We begin with the category of belief. As we have already indicated, we can learn much about belief from the way people perform rituals and the way in which they structure their communities. But for this section, we will focus on the beliefs themselves.

Your first task is to identify the central beliefs of your research group. The important step in this task is to make sure that you are identifying what *they* think is central, not what *you* think is most important. You might be very concerned, for example, about beliefs concerning the Bible, and you might assume that the most important beliefs for a religion concern how they view and interpret and use the Bible. But that may be a very minor concern for the group you are studying.

How can you begin to identify *their* central beliefs? There are several ways to do this. First, listen to what people are saying and doing during a service. For example, if they spend a lot of time reading from a particular book, or treat that book with reverence and continually refer to it, then something of importance is going on. Alternatively, if no mention is made of a particular concept or figure, then you might begin to question your earlier assumptions about its importance.

Second, check with members and leaders about what they think are the most important beliefs of their faith. You might ask someone to tell you what distinguishes members of this group from other religious people, or you might ask for a statement about the two or three most important beliefs shared by members of the congregation.

Third, find out whether there are explicit statements of belief that the community has developed. In Christianity, for example, several *creeds* have been written down and are recited at most services by members of the community. These documents attempt to set down, briefly and concisely, the central affirmations about the world and God that are shared by members of the church. If such documents are available, read them, and ask someone to read through them with you and explain any parts you do not understand.

Fourth, pay attention to the sort of language people use, both in their services and in speaking to you privately. Do they continually make references to God in their everyday speech, for example? Do they seem to draw rigid boundaries between their own group and others, such as by suggesting that anyone who does not agree with their beliefs is not saved?

As you proceed with your research, more and more questions will arise concerning the nature of the group's beliefs. You may not be able to fully understand what they believe, in part because there is usually a wide range of belief within any given community. Indeed, one important question you might want to ask repeatedly is, "Do most other members of this group share your belief about this?" Your goal is to gain a broad appreciation for what the major beliefs of the group are, how those beliefs are expressed, and what they seem to mean to some of the members.

One final word about belief. If you are a thoughtful person, you will probably find that some of your beliefs are being challenged or questioned as you conduct your research. Other people might begin to ask you why you don't share the group's belief, or you might wonder youself why your views are different and who is "right." While such self-questioning can be a very important and valuable result of such research, it is not the purpose of the research, and you should always try to separate out the research itself from such personal exploring. Remember that the question of whether or not these people are right or wrong, saved or not saved, is not relevant to conducting your research. You might be amazed that anyone could believe the way these people do; such amazement should drive you to work harder to figure out why such a belief would make sense, rather than leading you to dismiss the idea and the people as foolish.

If you are having trouble dealing with your own personal faith, or lack of it, as you proceed with the research, you might consider speaking to your instructor. Alternatively, seek out a religious leader in your own community and talk the matter over with that person. In any event, try to stay focused on the task of understanding how the beliefs shared by this group seem to make sense *for them* whether or not they make any sense to you.

Examples of religious beliefs and associated questions follow:

THE SACRED/GOD/DIVINITY

What do group members believe is the central object of religious faith?

If they believe in God, what do they mean by this term?

How is the sacred experienced by members of the community?

Are there certain statements of faith that all people in the community must accept?

RELIGIOUS AUTHORITY

What sources (either written or spoken) are used to tell people what is true?

If the Bible is important, how do the group members understand how the Bible was written? How literally do they read it? Do they believe it is without error ("inerrant")?

Which parts of the texts are particularly authoritative for the group? Why?

Are there figures in their religious tradition whose views are seen as authoritative? Who are these people? Why are they viewed in this way?

How important are the statements or beliefs of the major officials of the wider religious body, such as the denominational leaders?

SALVATION

Do members believe in heaven or hell, nirvana, or other concepts referring to a higher or lower state of existence? If so, what do such
terms mean to them?

Do they believe all people can be "saved"? What does this mean? Do
they believe they themselves are saved?

How do they weigh the relative importance of life in this world and life
beyond—if they believe in life beyond?

RELIGION AND ETHICAL ISSUES

What connections do they see between their religious beliefs and ethical issues?

How do they make ethical decisions about contemporary problems
(such as abortion, obedience to law, or euthanasia)?

How important do they believe questions of personal responsibility
are? Are members expected to act according to their own conscience,
even if that conflicts with the views of the religious authorities?

RELIGIOUS RITUAL

As you conduct your research, you are likely to be most drawn to questions about the ritual life of the community. This is natural, because such
elements are the most visible and often the most interesting feature of any
organized religious community.

You cannot possibly attend to everything that happens during the perfor-
mance of a religious ritual, simply because so much is going on. We suggest
that you begin by thinking of a few questions for yourself that come out of your
own experiences or interests, and make sure that you focus on *at least* these
few elements of the service. As you find yourself noticing other things, take
note of them as well; indeed, you might well find that you become more
fascinated by something you had never even thought of before. But drawing
up an initial list at least helps you avoid the feeling of complete foundering in
the midst of a strange experience.

We suggest a long list of such questions here. You will doubtless be able to come up with others that may be of more interest to you. We present this list only to help you begin to think about the aspects of religious ritual that may be interesting and worthy of study.

SYMBOLS

What religious objects or images are present in the place of worship? (Crosses, icons, seated Buddhas, etc.?) How are they presented? Where are they located in the sanctuary? What do they look like? (Draw pictures wherever possible to help yourself remember.)

How do these religious objects seem to function during the service? Do people look at them? Do they bow to them? Are the objects carried around during the service?

What is said explicitly about the objects during the service? Are they mentioned in readings or in sermons?

In looking at objects (including the building itself), try to distinguish between the following sorts of questions:

What is the purpose of the object? (To be worshipped? To be meditated upon? To hold or point to other symbols?)

What is the content or subject of the object? (The crucifixion of Jesus? The journeys of Muhammed? The seated Buddha?)

What is the placement of the object? (At the front of the congregation? Next to each pew? At the end of a busy street?)

What are the components of the object? (Wood? Brick and stone? Stained glass?)

How are the components arranged? (Building in the shape of a cross? Stained glass in a circle? Twelve statues placed around the church?)

When is the object used or focused upon? (Throughout a service? During a particular time in the service? Whenever people are silent?)

What does the object symbolize? (Jesus' death? The glory of God's house? The beauty of creation?)

How do you feel when you look at the object? (Moved? Confused? Afraid? Uplifted?)

ORDER OF THE SERVICE

What are the central elements of the service? Does the service have a formal structure?

How do the different sections of the service work together? Why does one part seem to follow another?

Which sections seem to be the most important to the members of the congregation?

How long is the service?

Who begins and ends the service? Is there a clear beginning and end?

LANGUAGE

What sort of language is used during the service? Is the service performed in English? If so, what type of English is used (everyday English, more formal language, Elizabethan language)?

Who does most of the speaking during the service?

How important is language in the service? Are there periods of silence or singing?

LEADERSHIP

Is there one person who leads the service? What is this person's role during the service? What tasks does he or she perform?

How distant is the leader from the other members? Does the person make contact with other people or walk down into the seating area?

What tone of voice does this leader use? What style of speaking and gesturing is used?

How do the members respond to the leader? Do they listen attentively?

SOUNDS

Other than speaking, what sounds are part of the service?

Is there any music? If so, what kind? Are any musical instruments played? Is there a choir?

Are there periods of silence during the service? If so, what effect do they seem to have, and what does their purpose seem to be?

CONGREGATION PARTICIPATION

In what ways does the congregation participate in the service?

Are there responsive readings?

Are there readings that are read in unison?

Do members of the congregation perform any of the main functions of the service, such as reading from the Bible or handing out or collecting anything, such as money? What are the characteristics (gender, race, dress, speaking skill, etc.) of the people who did participate? Are they representative of the congregation at large?

CONGREGATION BEHAVIOR

How would you describe the general behavior of most of the members of the congregation?

Did they pay attention to what was happening in the service?

Was there a lot of talking or whispering? Did people move around during the service?

Did most people arrive on time? Did some people come in late or leave early?

RELIGIOUS COMMUNITY

Finally, what are some of the questions you might ask about the religious community itself? Some of these questions are important simply as background information, to let the reader know who the members are and what sorts of people they seem to be. Other questions, however, are tied in much more closely with both belief and ritual.

Again, we merely offer some illustrative questions that you might want to look at in your observations. Some of the information might be gathered more easily in interviews or from literature provided by the community. But try your hand at gathering some of the material by observation.

The first set of questions deals with demographic or background information about the people who either attend a service or who belong to a congregation. Remember that these are two different populations; you might find that certain people are attending the service you observed, but they may not represent the members of the religious community as a whole. This is something to discuss with the group's leader or an informed staff member.

DEMOGRAPHIC INFORMATION

How old are the members of the congregation? (Make some rough estimates in percentage terms, if you can.)

What percentage are males, and what percentage females?

Are many children in attendance? What ages are they?

What ethnicity do most members seem to be?

Can you draw any conclusions about the social class background of people who are present? (You might make some guesses on the basis of dress, language, demeanor, number of children, and so on, and then check out your hunches by asking a staff member.)

In a service, you can try to estimate the percentage of people in each category in several different ways. If few people are present, a simple count will be easy. If there are too many people for that, you can try noting every tenth person, or the person at the end of each row. Another approach is to arrive early and keep track as people enter the building. (Remember our earlier cautions about writing too much down during the service, however.)

PHYSICAL STRUCTURE OF THE SETTING

Where is the building located? In what sort of neighborhood is it located? What other buildings surround it? What seems to be happening in the streets when you enter and leave?

What does the building look like? How new is it? How large is it? Is it well kept? Is it large enough for the number of people who seem to be using it?

Who else uses the building? Are there other religious services going on? Do any other organizations share the building with the religious group?

How "expensive" does the building seem to be? Are there fancy objects and decorations? Are there stained-glass windows?

What does the building seem to symbolize? Does the shape, size, construction, or "feel" of the structure convey certain religious attitudes or meanings?

GROUP ACTIVITIES

What activities other than religious services does the group engage in? (Many of these might be listed in the program handed out with the service, or mentioned during the service in an announcement period.)

How good is attendance at such other events? How much interest seems to be shown in such activities?

Are these activities performed with or for other members of the religion, or do they serve people from other traditions?

What is the nature of these other activities (for example, educational, health care outreach, social services, group prayer, political lobbying, entertainment, fund-raising)?

HISTORY OF THE GROUP

When was the religious group founded? When was the broader religious "denomination" of which it is a part first founded?

What is the current membership? Is membership rising or falling?

What have been significant shaping moments in the history of the congregation?

(Most of this information is best gathered in interviews with a group leader or staff member.)

ORGANIZATIONAL STRUCTURE

How is the group organized?

Who are the group's leaders? What sorts of power and responsibility do they have? How are they chosen? How long have they served in their current positions?

How active are the other members in deciding on group policies and practices? Are there committees or decision-making bodies composed of members?

Is the group connected with a wider denomination or religious community? If so, what is the nature of that connection? How much independence does the local group have in determining its policies and choosing its leaders?

How are new members selected and supported? Are there membership criteria?

How are current members disciplined? Are there ways to expel someone from the group? Has this ever happened?

CONCLUDING COMMENTS

As you ask questions and develop tentative answers, continue to think about the interactions among belief, ritual, and community. How do these three elements of religious experience work together, or at cross-purposes, for your particular religious group? As far as you can determine, which of the three seems to be most essential from the standpoint of the members, and which seems to be the source of the most trouble at the moment? (In other words, do people in the group disagree or argue most about differences in belief, ritual, or gaining new and active members?)

You do not need to focus on the same set of questions in every observation. Indeed, if you are reflecting on each of your experiences, you should find that you bring a somewhat different set of questions to each new observation, since you will be influenced by what you have learned (and been confused by!) in your last observation. This is as it should be; the process of research should be one of continually refocusing and refining your key themes and topics. The finished product may bear little or no resemblance to what you thought you were going to write about when you first appeared nervously at the door on that first visit.

A TROUBLESHOOTING GUIDE FOR OBSERVATIONAL RESEARCH

Because observational research is usually the most unpredictable and anxiety-ridden type of work for students, we have provided a brief list of potential problems that could arise and some suggested solutions and responses. It is extremely unlikely that any of these problems will arise in your project, but in case you are lucky (or unlucky) enough to encounter them, this guide may be helpful.

What should you do if one of the following happens?

1. *You are asked to join the organization you are studying.*

Thank the individual for the offer, and respond that you would like to learn more about the group but that you are here as part of a research project for a class. If the person persists, repeat the fact that you are not thinking of joining, that you are interested in learning about the group as part of a school project, and that you would be glad to learn more about the person's relationship with the group. A pleasant but forceful response will get your point across.

In general, treat the request as a piece of information that you can use to understand more about the group. For example, ask the person why he or she wants you to join, how many new members join each year, and what initiation ceremonies, if any, are performed for new members. By asking such questions, you can effectively deflect an uncomfortable personal encounter into one more interesting conversation about the group. Remember that, as with all your observations, the focus of your attention should be on the group and how its members feel and experience their world.

If you should run into someone who continues to try to get you to join, you may have to cut off the conversation politely by saying that you have another engagement, and leave. But such a step should be a last resort.

2. *You are in a service in which people are doing something that makes you uncomfortable.*

Try to stretch your own sense of what is "comfortable" when you attend services. You may never have kneeled at a service; see what it feels like. You might never have prayed out loud; try it to see what it feels like.

But—and this is an extremely important *but*—do not do anything that makes you feel that you are violating your own sense of what is right, or that makes you feel that you are being untrue to your own religious or ethical principles or beliefs. If the action feels this way, do not participate in it; just sit or stand quietly and observe what other people are doing.

3. *You are asked to do something you object to doing.*

Do not do it. Say politely that you would rather not do so. If you have not already done so, identify yourself as a nonmember who is present as part of a school research project. If the person persists, repeat what you have already said. In very rare circumstances, you might have to leave the service to avoid performing the action. There is nothing wrong with doing so; treat that as information you have gained. If the activity is one that is essential to any such service, you might have to select another religious group for your project; talk over the experience with your instructor.

4. *You are asked to leave the service.*

Leave the service. If possible, ask someone before you leave why you are being asked to leave. If this is not possible, make a phone call in a day or two, explain what happened, and indicate that you would like to know why you were asked to leave. Speak in a polite tone of voice; you are not challenging the group's right to ask you to leave; you merely want to understand why they did so.

5. *You think you might want to join the group.*

New experiences can be powerful and exciting, and you might be drawn to the group at a more personal level. Do not be afraid of such reactions; indeed, you should use them in your paper as very important data. Try to explain, to the reader and to yourself, precisely what attracts you to the group—what needs of yours are being met, what values are being realized, what goals are being achieved, what feelings are being brought forth.

But it is equally important to try to keep some perspective on the group, at least as long as you are writing the paper. Just as we recommended that you try not to study a group of which you are already a member, *we also believe that you should not join any group while you are studying it.* After your report is completed, of course, you might choose to return, talk to some members of the group, and make a decision about your own future relationship to this religion. But try to keep that decision somewhat separate from the research project you are engaged in.

6. *You are too nervous to attend a service.*

Follow our earlier recommendations about minimizing these fears: Write them down, ask a friend or two to come to the service with you, make a phone call to find out what to expect when you get there. If you take these steps, your anxiety will usually be lowered considerably. Also, remind yourself that everyone gets nervous entering a strange new situation, and there is nothing unusual about the way you feel. If possible, you can talk to a student who completed the assignment last year, and find out what the experience was like.

If you remain too afraid to proceed, speak with your instructor about the problem. Take your list of fears to your instructor, and go through the list point by point. Or show the list to a close friend or adviser, and ask that person to help you understand why you are afraid to attend. It is likely that such a conversation with a knowledgeable and sympathetic person will make you feel comfortable enough to proceed.

9
Interviewing

Let us assume that you have observed and participated until you are blue in the face, but you still cannot figure out what these people believe or why they conduct these strange rituals. You have counted how many people come to services and have calculated what proportion of them are women, but you don't know what the total membership of the group is. You have overheard snippets of conversation about the previous minister, but you haven't been told why he or she was fired.

Interviewing is an indispensable tool of social research, because it allows you to ask direct questions of people who know some pieces of the puzzle. You might want to discover what members believe, in which case your interview will center on personal beliefs and whether they are shared by other members. You might want to gather some general information about the congregation; if so, you can ask a knowledgeable person some straightforward questions about who belongs to this group. You might desire some historical information about the community's past, and you would then ask a longtime member to fill you in.

Interviews can occur at any time during a research study. Indeed, in a somewhat more informal way, you are already interviewing people when you ask the usher where to sit or when you chat with members after a service. In all such contacts, be polite, attentive, and open. These general rules apply to more formal interviews as well.

If you stop to think about it, you have probably been conducting interviews all of your life. When you asked a relative to tell you about his experiences fighting in a war; when you talked to a teacher about where you should go to college; when you asked a librarian to give you some help with a paper, you were interviewing. The crucial elements of any interview situation are very simple: (1) a person who needs some information that cannot be gained easily in any other way, (2) a person who knows something about that information, and (3) a context in which the person being interviewed feels comfortable sharing the information.

INTERVIEWING: WHO AND WHEN

Here are a few general guidelines in deciding who and when to interview.

1. INTERVIEW ONLY WHEN YOU CANNOT GATHER THE INFORMATION IN ANOTHER WAY.   If you can observe something for yourself, there is little point in wasting time (yours and the other person's) in an interview. Therefore, talk only to people who can give you something you don't already have.

2. INTERVIEW ONLY WHEN YOU KNOW WHAT YOU WANT TO ASK.   You might be wondering about the rituals of a community, but it makes no sense to interview someone before you have gone to a service yourself. After attending, you can ask about the meaning of specific rituals you observed, rather than having the person explain to you everything that happens at a service. The more focused your project is, the better your interviews will be.

3. SELECT PEOPLE IN DIFFERENT "SOCIAL LOCATIONS" TO INTERVIEW.   Speak to leaders, staff, members, and even visitors, if possible. Talk to long-term and short-term members, to people who are very active, and to some who are not. The broader your interview sample, the more accurate you will be about the group as a whole.

4. ASK THE APPROPRIATE QUESTIONS OF THE APPROPRIATE PEOPLE.   If you want a thorough exposition of the theology of the religious denomination, talk to the religious leader (priest, minister, rabbi, or whoever is in that role). If you want to assess the actual beliefs of some average members, interview some average members. If you want information about the budget, speak to a staff or administrative person. Don't waste your time by asking people what they don't know or what they know only secondhand.

5. ASK PEOPLE YOU INTERVIEW WHO ELSE YOU SHOULD INTER-VIEW.   At the end of every interview, make a habit of saying. "You have been very helpful. If there anyone else I would benefit from speaking to?" Allow the members to help define your interview list.

INTERVIEWING: HOW

Interviews can be thought of primarily as structured conversations. You should have a set of questions you want to ask and a general order in which you want to ask them. But you will gain more if you allow yourself to follow leads suggested by the person you are speaking to. If you don't end up asking all of your questions, that's fine, as long as what you did learn was helpful.

Interviews can be scheduled informally. Just call the person, indicate who you are and why you are studying the group, and say that you thought they might be able to help you answer some questions. Let them suggest a time to meet, and try to be flexible to fit into their schedule; remember, they are doing you a favor. Try to schedule at least thirty minutes for your first interview with each person, and more if they are willing to spend more time with you.

Develop an *interview schedule* before the interview. The next section of this chapter gives you some ideas about what kinds of questions to ask. Don't pack too many questions into a single interview. Separate the questions into two groups: (1) questions that are most important to ask this person, and (2) questions you would like to ask them if there is time. Plan to ask the first group of questions first.

You might want to "pretest" your interview on at least one or two people before going into the field. Ask a friend to act out the part of a member of a religious group, and role-play the interview, with your friend providing you with answers he or she makes up. At the end of the process, ask for advice about both the form and the content of the interview. Were the questions clear? Did the interview flow smoothly from point to point? Were overly sensitive areas covered? Using your friend's comments and your own sense of how it went, revise the interview plan.

Unless you are planning to tape-record the interviews, type out your interview guide with enough space between each question for you to write some notes as the interview proceeds. Photocopy several copies of the guide, and revise it periodically as needed. You will probably use a somewhat different set of questions for each interview, and you may add and subtract questions during the course of your research as your ideas become more focused.

At the very beginning of the interview session, you should cover two points. First, assure your respondents of complete confidentiality, if they desire it; that is, promise that you will not identify them personally, unless they have no objection to being identified. Remind them that you are interested only in learning what they think and believe, and that you will honor their privacy. In many instances, members of the clergy will not mind being quoted in your paper; members or lay leaders of the group may be more hesistant, especially if there is some controversy brewing in the organization.

Second, if you have decided to tape-record the interview, ask them if they are willing to have you use the machine. Assure them that no one else will hear the tapes and that you are doing this only so that you can be more accurate in analyzing your information and so that you don't have to scribble notes frantically while they are talking. Remind the respondents that you will turn off the tape recorder at any point if they desire. If they choose not to be taped, do not insist.

We strongly recommend taping your interviews whenever possible. A small tape recorder (preferably with a built-in microphone) can be purchased very inexpensively, and will come in handy in many situations. Most people have no objections to being taped, and almost everyone seems to forget the machine is even there after the first few minutes of the interview.

The following suggestions should help you develop interview questions and conduct the interview in a way that will maximize the validity and usefulness of the data:

1. **ASK QUESTIONS SIMPLY AND DIRECTLY.** Don't try to impress the person you are interviewing with how intelligent you are, how sophisticated your vocabulary is, or what great insight you have into the group. Don't use fancy phrases or technical terms, and use as few words as possible. (Ask, "How many members belong to this group?" not "How many people do you have who are presently involved as members of this particular group right now?") Be sure to determine what your interviewee means by the use of particular words; for example, the term *member* is defined differently by different groups, so you should ask how membership is determined if this is one of your issues.

2. **REMEMBER THAT YOU ARE CONDUCTING THE INTERVIEW.** Your goal is to learn what *they* know or think, not to tell them what *you* know or think. Interviewing is not an "equal conversation," and don't let it turn into one. Try to avoid giving your own opinions or feelings during the interview.

3. **MOVE FROM SIMPLE TO COMPLEX QUESTIONS.** Begin with some easier and descriptive questions (such as "How long have you been a member?"), and move to more penetrating and complex questions as you go along.

4. **ASK QUESTIONS IN A NEUTRAL FASHION, AVOIDING "LOADED" QUESTIONS AT ALL COSTS.** Ask, "What do you believe about the literal truth of the Bible?" rather than "Don't you believe the Bible is literally true?" Never start a question with a phrase such as "Do you agree that . . .,"

or "Isn't it true that . . .," or "Haven't you ever . . . ." These are probably the most commonly made mistakes in interviewing, and they are fatal. You want to find out what the other person honestly thinks, not what they think you want them to say.

5. AVOID AMBIGUOUS QUESTIONS.   For example, if you ask, "How religious is your family?" your respondent is unlikely to know what you are referring to. (Attendance at services? Depth of religious belief? Payment of dues? Private prayer?) You will have no way to interpret the answer, anyway. If you want to know about prayer, ask about prayer.

6. DON'T USE DOUBLE QUESTIONS.   Avoid asking questions such as "Are you active in this congregation and in agreement with the beliefs of the group?" A "yes" answer to such a question doesn't allow you to know which part of the question is being responded to. Be very careful to ask one question at a time.

7. AVOID QUESTIONS WITH CLEAR EMOTIONAL OR CULTURAL VALUES ATTACHED TO THEM.   You might not be able to avoid all such questions, but be aware of the possibility that the person is telling you what is the "accepted" answer. Questions about belief in God, happiness in marriage, and support for values such as peace and justice seldom elicit very interesting responses in the type of research you are doing. Probe beneath the surface by asking what the person believes about God, or how the religious tradition would help in solving a particular social problem.

8. BE INVOLVED BUT OBJECTIVE.   This is a very delicate balance to find, and people have very different styles of interviewing. In general, we recommend that you show interest in what you are being told, but that you try not to reveal your own likes or dislikes about what people say. Feel free to laugh if they make a joke, but only if you are positive that they are trying to be funny. Give neutral feedback by using both verbal and nonverbal cues. For example, say, "Oh, yes," "I see," or "That's interesting" periodically. Maintain eye contact, nod your head occasionally, and don't fidget or play with your pen or the tape recorder.

9. ASK FOLLOW-UP QUESTIONS.   The mark of an excellent interviewer is not so much in deciding upon the initial questions, but in knowing how and when to probe more deeply. If you don't understand what someone has said, ask for clarification. If you are wondering what lies behind a particular comment, ask for elaboration. Phrases such as the following will be helpful: "Could you tell me a bit more about that?" and "I'm interested in why you think people believe that."

10. ASK FOR SPECIFIC EXAMPLES AND ACTIONS. People love to talk in generalities; the problem for you is that, if this is all you have, your paper will be written in generalities as well. Whenever possible, get people to give you examples of what they are saying. Ask them: "Could you give me an example of what you meant when you said that people here are very religious?" "When was the last time you saw someone praying for someone else?" "What topics did the minister cover in her last couple of sermons?" The more specific you can get your respondents to be, the more you will know about the organization and the richer your evidence will be.

11. USE THE PROPER TERMS IN ASKING QUESTIONS. Don't ask, "Who is your minister?" when interviewing in a Jewish congregation, for example. If you are unsure of the appropriate terms, either read about the group before the interview or confess your ignorance, saying something like the following: "I want to ask you about your religious leaders—by what title do you refer to them?"

12. RELAX. Interviewing can be difficult and draining, but your goal is to put the people at ease and give them time and space to tell you what they think and know. Don't be in too much of a hurry to move on to the next question; pauses can be very useful, providing a chance to think more about what has just been said. When someone finishes an answer, but you think there might be more to be said, wait a few seconds before rushing in with your next question; sometimes, such silence can be very creative.

13. WITHIN REASON, TRY TO MOVE THE INTERVIEW TOWARD YOUR INTERESTS. You will want to be sensitive to people's desire to talk about certain things, and you want to allow them to tell you what they want to tell you. But keep in mind that this is *your* interview, in the service of *your* project. If the interview seems to be drifting off track (and in a direction that you don't find helpful for your purposes), you might try to get it back by saying something like this: "This is fascinating, and I would love to hear more about it sometime, but I have a few other questions I wanted to ask you." Don't feel like you have to let the person ramble on endlessly.

14. ABOVE ALL, *LISTEN*. This is perhaps the single most important word of advice we could give about the art of interviewing. Listen to what the person is telling you and how it is being told. Don't assume you know the answers beforehand, or even that you are sure that you are asking the right questions. Allow the other person's perspective to guide you.

To help you adopt this perspective, we suggest the following strategy. Try pretending that you are an anthropologist on a field study in a totally foreign culture; or, if you are a science-fiction fan, imagine that you are a

Martian who has been sent to earth to try to understand what human beings are doing in these strange groups called religious organizations. In this way, treat your interviewees as "informants," people who are going to help you make sense of this strange situation and world. You will listen, because you are the outsider who needs to be told how things work.

You can adopt this approach mentally, but you can also share it with the person you are interviewing. Early in the interview, you might consider saying something like the following: "You know, I really don't know very much about this group yet, and I really hope you can give me some better insight into what it is like to be a member. I hope you'll excuse any mistakes I might make in asking questions, but I really do want to understand what it is like from your perspective." You can even repeat a shortened version of this comment periodically during the interview, if this seems appropriate. Such comments remind the interviewees that you are an outsider and that you want them to give you an honest view of the insider's perspective.

INTERVIEWING: WHAT

What should you ask in the interview? As we have already indicated, you will need to develop a unique set of questions to fit your particular research interests, the nature of the group under investigation, and the individual being interviewed. We can, however, suggest some types of questions, with examples of each type, to help you develop your own interview format.

Members

Here are some sample topics and questions for interviews with members in religious settings.

BACKGROUND INFORMATION

How long have you been a member of this group?

Tell me a little about why you joined.

Are other members of your family involved in the group? [If yes] Who? How active are they?

What sort of religious upbringing did you have?

EXPERIENCES WITH THE GROUP

What do you like best about this group? (Ask for specifics.)

What do you like least about it? (Ask for specifics).

What has been your most positive experience with the group so far?

What has been your most negative or disappointing experience with the group?

Are some of your best friends also members? If so, how many?

What activities do you take part in regularly?

RELIGIOUS BELIEFS

What are the central beliefs shared by members of this religious community?

What are your own personal beliefs about

whether the Bible is literally true?

the meaning of personal salvation?

the proper role of your religious community in solving social problems?

Clergy

Here are some questions that you might want to ask the clergy about themselves.

CLERGY

Personal background:

How long have you been in your present position here?

Why did you decide to become a [appropriate term for *leader*]?

Where did you receive your religious training?

Why did you choose this particular [denomination/religion]?

Have you had other positions in other religious groups? [If yes] Tell me about them.

Tell me about your own family (brothers, sisters, parents, etc.).

In addition, many of the following questions about the group you are studying should be put to the clergyperson whom you interview.

Group History

I'd appreciate if you could give me a brief history of this [church/synagogue/temple/mosque].

When was it founded?

What pattern of growth or decline has occurred?

Have any important events occurred recently in this religious community?

Group Characteristics

How would you describe your congregation?

What are its special features?

What makes it distinctive from other religious groups in the area?

How would you describe the members? [Ask about ethnicity, social class, education, type of employment, commitment to the group, age, etc.]

Religious Beliefs

What would you say are the two or three most central beliefs of this religious community? [Probe for explanation and elaboration.]

What are your personal beliefs about [nirvana, human suffering, salvation, the divinity of Jesus, the infallibility of the Bible]? (You will have to decide what the relevant terms are for your particular group, of course.)

How would you describe the seriousness of religious belief of most of your members?

What questions about belief do members of your community most frequently ask?

Depending on the amount of time that you are granted for the interview, you may want to explore some of the following questions—or perhaps reserve them for a second interview.

Group Activities

What do you believe are the most important goals for this community to achieve?

How much involvement does your group have in [social action programs, interfaith dialogues, ecumenical activities, missionary work]?

Can you suggest any programs or activities that I should attend to understand your group better?

Group Organization

How are policy decisions made within your [church/synagogue/temple/mosque]?

What is the chain of command, if there is one?

What role do you personally play in the decisions?

How were you first chosen to be the clergyperson here?

What sorts of connections does this [church/synagogue/mosque] have with other members of your religion?

Do not feel that you are limited to asking just these questions, or that you can easily ask all of them in any single interview. Pick the sorts of questions that interest you the most and the ones your interviewee can best answer. You may flounder occasionally, asking something the person doesn't know; even the most practiced interviewers do that occasionally. Every question does not need to elicit a fascinating (or even useful) response; however, with luck and some skill, every interview will provide you with some unique and interesting information.

CONCLUDING THE INTERVIEW

When the interview is over, thank the person for being willing to talk with you, and if they have requested that their identity not be disclosed in your report, repeat your assurances about the confidentiality of the interview. Ask them whether there are other people they would suggest you speak to, and write down their names (and phone number, if they can provide them). If the interview has been helpful and you think you might like to continue the conversation, ask whether the person might be willing to meet with you again after you have conducted more of your research. If they are willing, make a note of this, get a phone number, and say that you may be in touch soon.

When you leave, be sure to thank any other people (staff, family, etc.) who helped you arrange the interview.

CONCLUDING COMMENTS

The next chapter will help you determine what to do with the information from the interviews you have conducted. The quality of your analysis and the final product are dependent upon the quality of the data, however, so you can save yourself an enormous amount of time and energy by planning and conducting the interviews in a systematic and intelligent fashion. The more organized you are in choosing people to interview, focusing your questions on the topics you want to discuss, and in asking and probing in ways that draw out the most thorough and valid responses from the people you speak to, the easier it will be to write your paper, and the more valuable your conclusions and insights will be.

Do not look at interviewing as work that is "preliminary" to the writing of the paper. Interviews, as observations, are the very core of the research and should be approached carefully and thoughtfully. But they also can be enormously enjoyable; after all, you have the opportunity to sit down with strangers and find out how their minds work, what they think and worry about, how their world is organized, and what they would like to change. If you choose topics in which you are genuinely interested and select your interview subjects carefully, interviewing will be both stimulating and fun.

10
Analyzing the Data

PROBING AND REASSESSING
AND PROBING AND REASSESSING . . .

The best way to perform your research is to move back and forth continually between actual investigation and thoughtful assessment. Once you have arrived at your initial questions and method, make your phone calls and conduct your observations, as appropriate. After each foray into the field, however, step back, look at the questions again, and begin to refine and rethink the way in which you are asking them and what you will need to answer them.

For instance, you might find after attending a meeting and speaking with a couple of people that there are several layers of organizational authority, including clergy, committees, and part-time chairpersons or coordinators. Such a finding might interest you in various ways, and you could rework your focus accordingly. You might be most interested in exploring the distinction between ordained persons (clergy) and nonordained members, to see what sorts of influence or control the first group of people have. Or, you might be more interested in the ways the different committees interact with each other, and how any overarching group (such as a vestry or board of directors) functions to hold them together.

Depending on which of these questions interest you, the next stage of your research would be focused on this new issue. If you chose the ordained/laity focus, then you would want to have extensive interviews with the leaders in both groups, and the focus of the interviews would revolve around their respective training, background, and influence. If your new focus was the organizational layout, then your next step of research would call for attendance at several meetings and interviews with the heads of the groups to ask them how their piece fits in with all the others. You would then go back and conduct a few of these interviews or observations, and then sit down again and see whether the questions were now focused in a new direction.

This back-and-forth process should continue until you have enough information to answer your questions, which are now very focused. By this time, if you have followed the analytical suggestions we will make later on in this chapter, you should have a detailed outline of the paper already in hand.

The goal of this process is to view your research as an ongoing and cyclical process of thinking, analyzing, and field work, with each of these steps moving you along to the next stage.

MANAGING YOUR FIELD NOTES

Whenever you make an observation, conduct an interview, or talk informally with someone about your project, you should consider this as a piece of data that both leads you back to your questions and serves as the basis for your eventual research report. If you are conscientious about your work, you will have more information than you can remember, and you should begin preparing for the task of organizing and analyzing the data. Therefore, you need to develop a system for keeping up with all this information as you go along.

You will probably have various types of notes as you proceed with your field work. Some thoughts will be jotted down on napkins and bulletins during services or meetings, while others will be more extensive notes taken after meetings or while reflecting on your experiences. In any event, get into the habit of writing down some form of notes on *every* experience you have, even if it is only a phone call to determine the time of a meeting.

Within a few hours of any observation or interview, sit down—preferably at a computer—and write extensive notes about what you experienced. Pay more attention to what happened than to what it means, although it is a good idea to jot down other reflections and interpretations as well. The following sorts of information should be part of these extensive notes.

INFORMATION THAT SHOULD BE IN FIELD NOTES

1. The date, time, place, purpose, and nature of the observation

2. A chronology, as well as you can remember it, of what happened

3. Who said what, and to whom

4. What the room or space looked and felt like to you

5. How people were acting (for example, fidgeting, paying attention)

6. The tone of the meeting or event (for example, lighthearted, serious)

7. What people were wearing

8. How you felt as the observation or interview progressed

Appendix 3 provides some more specific examples of what your notes might look like.

For interviews, you should type out a very detailed account of each of your questions and the person's response. If you took notes, try to replicate what the person said as precisely as possible. If you taped the interview, transcribe the entire interview (that is, type out word-for-word what was said) if you have time; if you don't have time, listen carefully to the entire tape and write down summaries of each answer, including direct quotations of responses to the most important questions you asked.

As you write out these notes, you will find yourself taking better notes during the actual observations or interviews. The more detailed your field notes are at the time, the more thorough you can be later in recollecting what you learned.

As we indicated, you do not have to restrict your field notes to information you actually learned at the time. It is useful to keep a separate set of notes where you can draw out your own interpretations, hunches, and guesses about what the information means and how you will use it in your final report. For example, if you attended a meeting in which the leader did most of the talking, your field notes should reflect this and should provide evidence (such as the approximate number of minutes the leader talked, or the range of issues on which that person expressed an opinion) to support such a conclusion. Your other set of notes could begin to interpret this finding. What do you think this says about the group? What does this suggest about how the group understands authority? Who else should you talk to in trying to understand this fact?

As you move closer to the actual writing stage, you should be spending more and more time on these interpretative reflections and note-taking. As long as you distinguish between these reflections and your reporting of what you observed, the entire package comprises your set of field notes and will be important when you sit down to organize and write your paper.

Be sure to include your personal feelings in these notes as well. It is important not to ignore your attraction to the group, your sense of embarrassment, or your impressions of disgust or distrust. Rather than pretend that these feelings do not exist, use them in your notes as a way to begin to ask about the meaning of what you are seeing and hearing. You may find that such intangible feelings suggest new and important ways to look at your questions.

Appendix 2 provides some suggestions for using a computer to organize your field notes. If you don't have a computer, you can organize your notes in whatever way is most useful to you. In this section, we suggest one approach that is helpful for many students. Feel free, of course, to adapt it to your own needs. Whatever method you use, the most important goal is to be able to keep a thorough record of what you have learned, and to begin to organize that material in a way that will aid the writing process.

Whether you are typing or writing out your field notes, you can use the following supplies to organize what will quickly become a large and unwieldy stack of papers: index cards (3 × 5, or 4 × 6), a group of file folders or a file with separate sections, a pair of scissors, and either carbon paper or a photocopy machine. The following steps will allow you to keep some degree of control over your information as you are conducting your research.

MANAGING FIELD NOTES

1. Each time you observe a meeting, conduct an interview, or read something about your group, place the notes for that event in a separate file folder. On the tab of the folder, clearly identify the nature of the observation and the date. Keep this material in a separate place, apart from the other notes you will be writing.

2. Make at least two copies of each of these field notes, including transcripts or descriptions of interviews and notes from books, articles, or documents you have read.

3. Read through your field note and code each paragraph in the margin according to topic. (For example, "history of the group" might be labeled as topic A, "ritual" as topic B, and "organizational structure of the group" as topic C.)

4. If you are writing your notes on pieces of paper, cut up one copy of the notes into separate strips of paper according to the different topics to which they correspond. Mark each strip of paper so that you will know which interview or observation it came from. (You will therefore have a separate strip of paper for each separate piece of data on any given subject; you may well have several strips from each observation, since you will probably learn something about several topics from that one event.)

If you are using index cards (which are much easier to handle), you will not have to cut anything, provided you remember to limit yourself to one substantive point on each index card.

5. Separate the strips of paper (or index cards) into file folders corresponding to each topic. For example, one folder would include all the notes referring to history of the group, no matter which observation, interview, or material this was drawn from.

The advantages of following such a systematic (and time-consuming!) procedure will be obvious to you only when you sit down to begin writing the paper. You will be able to reach for a folder and find all of your many notes on any given topic. The effort will be worth it.

To make sure that you are moving along in a coherent direction, we strongly recommend that you review your field notes at least once a week. Try to choose a set time on a regular basis when you can quietly go over what you have gathered so far, and add to the notes with further reflections and refinements as you read through your files. As you do this, you will be asking yourself not only what you have learned so far, but also what other information you need to gather to answer the questions that are now most important and interesting to you. As you get new insights, write these down and add them to the appropriate files, creating new files whenever necessary.

In addition to your topical files, you might create a separate file to serve as a developing outline for the final report. This file should include your reflections on the central focus as it develops, and you should even try to write out a tentative outline of the paper as a way to identify the remaining holes in your data. As you do this, you may find that the focus of the topic changes or that you are not quite as clear on some points as you thought you were. But that is precisely the point; it is far better to identify such changes and confusion while you are still conducting the research rather than on the night before the paper is due.

A final point about managing your field notes is in order. Remember that these are *confidential* papers and that you are therefore responsible for their protection. Leave people's names off the notes, unless your respondents have agreed to allow you to use their names in your report. (Develop a coding system to assign each person a created name or number, and keep a separate list of this code.) Don't show the research notes to your friends, and keep all research materials in a secure place.

ANALYSIS AND DISTINCTIONS

One of the key tasks a researcher confronts in analyzing large amounts of information is to find categories or groups into which to place the information. Once you have focused on a theme and have begun to ask (and answer) some of the key questions you are asking, the data seem to sit there as an undigested lump; your goal is to impose some conceptual order on this hodgepodge of material.

The most helpful way to begin to do this is to try to find some distinctions that can be applied to your information. The nature of these distinctions will depend on your particular questions and the type you have gathered. Let's follow our earlier example, however, to provide some idea of what such distinctions might look like.

Let's assume that your central theme was the nature of religious authority, and the questions involved the sort of role the leader played in the group. As you gathered information, you found that most people reported that the two leaders of the group exert almost complete control over policy decisions, while a few people told you that they have a lot of influence as well. Similarly, when you attended group meetings, you found that the leaders are very influential in some committees but that there is much more group participation in other situations. How could you begin to bring some order to such a wealth of information?

If you look carefully at the information described, you will notice that there are several different ways to divide up the data. The goal is to divide it in ways that are both interesting and revealing of what is actually there. (Remember our earlier comments about validity; the standard is a set of distinctions that reflect the different opinions and experiences in your research.)

To begin with, there is an obvious distinction between a participatory and a nonparticipatory style of organizational structure. You are probably familiar with several terms that attempt to capture this distinction: *democratic, egalitarian,* and *open* are several terms applied to the more participatory style, while terms such as *authoritarian, hierarchical,* and *closed* suggest the opposite. You can draw on such concepts in your reading, picking the ones that seem to best reflect the differences you have found. Alternatively, you can make up some terms of your own to capture this distinction.

But this is not the only type of categorization uncovered in this data. As we have described it, the data report some situations in which one tendency predominates, and others in which the opposite is found. What are the natures of these types of situations? As part of the analysis, you would form two groups: one consisting of all your observations that point toward the more participatory pole, the other made up of observations falling on the other end of the continuum. Look at these two sets, and try to figure out what elements each group has in common. Are those in one group made up of formal meetings, whereas the other consist of descriptions of informal gatherings or one-to-one encounters? Are the more participatory examples all cases in which a clergyperson was not present, whereas the others are those situations in which such a leader was present?

You might find several different explanations; so much the better. For each one that seems plausible, give a label of some sort to each category, and a broad term to describe the nature of the distinction. For example, if the first of our suggestions seems to make sense of the data, then you might call one type "formal meetings" and the other "informal encounters," and your continuum or dimension could be called "formality of interaction."

A simple diagram of the analysis you have just performed would look like this:

DIMENSION: FORMALITY OF INTERACTION

Formal Meetings   Informal Encounters

Example 1   Example 4

Example 2   Example 5

Example 3   Example 6

In some cases, dividing the information up into such groups might not work. You might have some leftover examples that don't fit into either one. When that happens, there are two strategies you can employ. First, rethink the nature of your categories and ask whether they might be helpfully broadened or redefined so as to encompass all of your cases. If this does not work, then consider creating a third (or fourth or fifth) category that represents a different point along the continuum. In our example, you might need to distinguish between one-to-one encounters and spontaneous activities or meetings, rather than simply putting all such cases together.

For each dimension, how many categories should you have? That depends on the distinction, as well as the variety of your data. In general, however, remember that point of this enterprise is to bring some order, coherence, and intelligibility to the information. If you have fifteen pieces of information, creating ten categories is not likely to help anyone understand what is going on. As a general rule, try to find no more than three or four categories for each distinction, if only because it is very hard for people to hold more than that number in their minds when they are reading your report.

There are still other sorts of distinctions you could draw out of your data. How about the question of who describes the organizational style in each way? Do men tend to believe that decision making is very open, while women believe the opposite? Do more active members feel one way, while less active people respond differently? Do older people respond differently than younger ones? Do newer members respond differently than long-term members?

This is where your imagination and creativity have an opportunity to flower. Think about all the possible distinctions that might explain such a difference, and try them out on your information. If they do not fit, make a note of that fact and move on to another possibility. When you find one that does help distinguish between the groups, make a note of it, try to figure out why that might be the case, and then move on to the next possibility. You may find several such distinctions, all of which help you understand the diversity of what you have found.

For each distinction that seems to point to something interesting in your data, start a separate file and begin to explore what you might say about it. Read over your other notes to see whether there are other hints or suggestions that would support or undermine that distinction. Consider theories or distinctions that appear in your course reading or lecture notes, and try them on for size. Write out some of your own thoughts about each distinction, not only about the evidence you have to support it, but also about what it might mean, how you might explain it, and what its significance is.

In creating your categories, be sure to write down the criteria you are using to allocate people or comments to each category. For example, why did you decide that five examples fall under the heading of formal meetings, while the other six fall under the heading of informal encounters? Forcing yourself to be explicit about creating categories has two important benefits: First, it will help you make sure that you have good reasons for drawing these distinctions; and second, you will have to include in your final paper some information concerning how and why you created each of these categories.

As you analyze and reanalyze your information in this way, keep reminding yourself that no one else has ever assembled precisely this set of data before. It is unique, and your analysis is unique. It is up to you to determine which theories fit the data, which distinctions make sense out of what is going on, which categories are of most use in understanding the distinctions. But also remember that many other people have analyzed similar sets of data, and therefore you can find much helpful reflection and suggestions from their work.

CONCLUDING COMMENTS

By the time you have completed the analysis, you should be ready to write your paper in a very straightforward manner. You will have a large set of folders, each containing numerous examples of a topic, theme, or distinction you have discovered. In addition, you will have a folder filled with notes to yourself about how to organize the paper, including outline suggestions and examples to use in each section. If you have followed these suggestions carefully and methodically, the paper will almost "write itself."

The most important point to emphasize in all we have said about analysis is that analysis begins at the moment you first gather any information and continues in an uninterrupted fashion until your paper is completed. Continually ask yourself about themes, distinctions, categories, and how to interpret them; keep reworking the data to find better or clearer ways to organize and understand what you are learning. If a distinction takes account of 90 percent of your observations, spend some time trying to account for that remaining nagging 10 percent.

Analysis is difficult, challenging, and frustrating. It is easier to sit down and count observations, or ask a series of questions, or read through some documents, than it is to try to figure out what all of this mass of information *means*. But that is the excitement and fun in conducting social research. The skills, the creativity, the imagination you bring to your analysis will help you think clearly about the world around you. The research paper you produce as a result will therefore be "yours" in a highly original and fulfilling way. The more energy and thought you put into your analysis, the stronger your paper will be and the more it will reveal of your own personality and thinking.

section four
WRITING YOUR PAPER

11

Getting Started

We cannot hope to teach anyone how to write a research paper in a single section of a short book. But we also cannot leave you in the lurch, sitting there with a set of file folders and a blank piece of paper in your typewriter. This section is written mainly for those people who need some pointers or reminders on how to organize and write a paper. If you have major problems with such projects, seek out your instructor or a writing advisor on your campus for further help.

There are three basic stages in translating your analysis into a final written document: organizing, writing, and editing. All three are equally essential and should be given the appropriate amount of time. Therefore, the first basic rule of writing your paper is to allow enough time to organize, write, and edit. These tasks cannot be done in an evening; that is, they cannot be done *well* in an evening, and we assume that, after spending all this time doing your research, you want to write a paper that is informative, clear, and insightful.

Your paper will be stronger if you are aware of the writing process when you first begin your research. Therefore, we urge you to read this section before beginning your work.

THE AUDIENCE FOR YOUR PAPER

In any writing project, it is important to know who the *audience* is. Your research paper is being written for your professor, who is usually the only intended reader. You may, of course, show the paper to other people (such as friends or relatives), but your teacher is the key person for whom it is being prepared. This fact has several important consequences for both the style and content of the way you write the paper:

1. Follow any specific suggestions or requirements you are given. This includes restrictions about the length, subject matter, organization, and style. If you find contradictions between your professor's suggestions and those provided in this book, *ask*. When in doubt, you are probably better off following the explicit suggestions of your professor, since he or she is the person who will respond to (and probably grade) your paper.

2. You can assume that this reader is an intelligent and well-read person. Do not be afraid to use technical terms, historical references, or theoretical concepts in the paper. However, you should always be clear about how you are using such terms.

3. Bear in mind that the reader is also receiving other papers, and that he or she is under serious time constraints to read and respond to your work. This means that it is even more important to present a clear and well-organized report that can be read easily and quickly. A close friend might be willing to read through a mishmash of thoughts and experiences, but your professor will not.

4. Finally, take into account what you know from your class about the professor's orientation and approach. This does *not* mean that you should try to figure out what the professor wants you to say and then just repeat that information in your paper. But it does mean that you might want to be particularly sensitive to certain themes and opinions you are expressing, clarifying your own views. For example, if your professor has a tendency to focus on the importance of philosophical ideas and logical arguments in discussing various religious groups, and you find yourself convinced that the less rational and more aesthetic aspects of the religious group are in fact most important for the members, you could include an additional paragraph in the paper indicating why you have arrived at this conclusion, in order to remind the professor that you are aware of other issues. Do not be afraid to disagree with what your professor has said in class. If you do disagree, however, be sure to provide supporting arguments and evidence for why and how you have arrived at your own position.

ORGANIZING

If you have analyzed your field research effectively, or if your project is based on library research and you now have a large stack of note cards in front of you, then the organization of the paper should be a relatively easy task. The first step is to write an outline of the paper you are about to produce.

Your instructor may have provided you with some guidelines concerning how the paper should be written and what format it should take. As usual, follow those guidelines if they conflict with what we say here. All we will do is give you some general suggestions that are appropriate for most research papers of this type.

An outline should be detailed enough to include every argument you will make, every issue you will discuss, and every conclusion you will draw. But it should not be so detailed that it includes every example or quotation you will use. Try to think of the outline as the skeleton on which you will hang the flesh of the paper—or, for those of you less biologically inclined, you might think of the outline as a musical theme upon which you embellish and develop melodies, counterpoints, and subtle harmonies.

How long should your outline be? There is no fixed length, just as there is no fixed length for your paper (although, again, your instructor may have some general guidelines). Assuming you are going to be writing a paper of about twenty pages, a good outline would usually be no more than two pages. Remember, of course, that the more detailed your outline is, the easier it will be to write the first draft of the paper. When in doubt, err on the side of a more extensive outline.

You are probably familiar with the form of an outline. The content will depend on your particular research project, of course. Here is what an outline of the project should cover. Note that this is not itself an outline for a paper; the completed outline would include the substance of each line, according to the content of the paper. For example, the outline would not read "Purpose of project," but "Purpose: Understand lines of authority in the Presbyterian church."

As you read through this formal outline example, notice the various key components, including introductory remarks, key themes and illustrations, and concluding comments.

ELEMENTS OF A SAMPLE TERM PAPER OUTLINE

I. Introduction
   A. Purpose of project
   B. Choice of particular group
   C. Key themes to be discussed in paper

II. Methods
   A. Observations
     1. Why conducted

2. How many, and when

3. Problems encountered

B. Interviews

1. Why conducted

2. How many, and when

3. Problems encountered

C. Other methods used

1. Written documents consulted

2. Other people consulted

III. Major theme of paper

A. Topic defined

B. Major types found in the group

C. Possible explanationns

D. Analysis supporting or discounting each explanation

IV. Other themes

V. Conclusion

A. Summary of major findings of paper

B. Suggestions for future research

C. What I learned from the project

Your actual outline may not include all of these elements, depending on the nature of your project.

You will know if your outline is complete enough when you sit down to begin writing your first draft. If you are unable to move fairly easily from topic to topic, return to the outline and think more carefully about the order in which you want to proceed.

The outline should be written as soon as possible and should be revised periodically. It is a good idea to try writing an outline when you begin your research, if only to determine how unclear you are at that point about your direction. Keep revising it as you gather more information and focus your topic. You will doubtless drop some sections, add others, reorganize the topics, and find holes that need to be filled with more research.

You do not need to include the outline itself in your final draft, unless your instructor asks you to do so. But the outline will provide the basis for the table of contents of the paper, as well as continually prod you to determine whether your paper is well organized and complete.

DEVELOPING ARGUMENTS

Much of your paper will be descriptive, answering questions such as: What do people believe? What is the history of the group? What did you see? What happened? How did you feel? But there will be some places where you are likely to be using these descriptions to make specific points, to develop positions and opinions and even theories about what you have discovered. How do you go about doing this in a written form?

In the broadest sense, what is involved here can be seen as "framing an argument." Arguments, in this sense of the word, are not necessarily disagreements or brutal verbal battles. Rather, an argument is a logical set of statements designed to convince someone that something is true. But there is an important reason why the word has the more "confrontational" meaning in our everyday language: The strength of an argument depends not merely upon whether it is in fact true, but on how well it is able to counter or defend itself against objections and counterclaims that might be brought against it.

There are several key requirements for a sound and convincing argument. Ask yourself each of these questions as you organize and prepare to make each point in the paper:

1. **IS THE ARGUMENT CLEAR?**   Nothing will be convincing if the reader cannot understand it. Be sure to specify all of the key terms you are using, and make each statement as concise as possible. If you are arguing that the religious leader is obeyed because of his or her personality, specify what *personality* means.

2. **IS THERE A CLEAR CONCLUSION OR POINT TO THE ARGUMENT?**   You may have mustered a lot of evidence, but unless it leads somewhere, it is not an argument.

3. **IS THE EVIDENCE THAT POINTS TO THE CONCLUSION VALID?**   If you have misinterpreted what you say or misused what people have told you, the entire argument will fall apart. A conclusion is only as valid as the facts or observations used to support it.

4. **ARE THE CONNECTIONS BETWEEN THE EVIDENCE AND THE CONCLUSION APPROPRIATE?**   Include only the data that are essential to lead to the conclusion, and be explicit about how each observation or piece of evidence leads to the conclusion.

Also, be sure that there is a logical connection between the evidence and the conclusion. For example, remember that causal relationships need to be in the correct temporal order to be plausible. It might appear that a leader with a lot of education is highly charismatic, but it would be a weak argument to suggest that the education creates the charisma. It is far more likely that the process works the other way around—that is, that people with stronger personalities might be more likely to become leaders, and leadership may require advanced education.

5. ARE THERE OTHER CONCLUSIONS THAT MIGHT BE DRAWN FROM THE SAME EVIDENCE? This is one of the hardest questions, but it is also one of the most important. Your argument will be undercut if someone can respond: "Yes, I agree with all the evidence, but there is another, equally believable explanation for what you have seen or heard." For example, you might be arguing that the leader's personality is responsible for his authority, but someone might suggest that it is, in fact, the leader's age or occupation or knowledge of texts that really provides the basis for being followed. If your evidence merely shows that the leader is followed, this will not convince anyone that your conclusion is better than the alternatives.

How do you address this problem? There is only one way—by rethinking the argument. Do you have any evidence that can be understood only in terms of your conclusion? To use our example, perhaps there are other people of the same age in the congregation, but who don't seem to have the same charismatic presence as the leader. If you can document this fact, it serves as a piece of evidence arguing for your conclusion against the alternative explanation that age is really the key factor.

You may find that, on reflection, you really cannot rule out other explanations on the basis of your evidence. That is fine; indeed, there is nothing wrong with presenting several alternative explanations, noting that your evidence does not eliminate any of them, but simply stating your own hunch about which one is more correct. If you do this, of course, you have not really presented an argument, but it is far better to be aware of what you can in fact conclude on the basis of your data, than go overboard and try to make a case for something that is easily shot down.

It is more likely, however, that your reflection on the alternative explanations will lead you back to your data, or even back to the setting to gather some more information. (This is one of the great advantages of beginning work on your project early enough to gather additional evidence while you are actually organizing your report.) Try to figure out what sort of evidence "counts" in favor of your own explanation, and whether your earlier interpretations might need to be reconsidered. In the process, you might even decide that one of the other explanations is better than the one you started with, in which case the argument presented in the paper could focus on the new one. (Isn't if fortunate that no one has access to the earlier drafts of our papers?)

Let's take another simple example. On the basis of your readings (and observations, if your paper includes field research), you may now believe that American Buddhists have a very distinct manner of worshipping, and that this type of practice (meditation) stems from certain understandings of the nature of the sacred. But someone else might respond to your claims by saying that other American religious groups (such as the Society of Friends) also use silent meditation in their services, and that the real reason for the use of this practice is not theological but psychological—that is, that certain types of individuals are more comfortable looking inside themselves than saying or singing collectively.

If you can recognize these potential counterarguments, you can begin to answer them. You might point them out in your paper, and then try to find some evidence (in your readings or field notes) that would support either your interpretation or the alternative. In the process, you might well decide that the new interpretation is stronger, in which case *that* can then become your own argument.

6. IS THE CONCLUSION BASED ON DIFFERENT SORTS OF EVIDENCE? An argument is always strengthened, not only by the amount of data supporting it, but by the diversity of types of data that can be used in its defense. If you can put together an argument about a leader's authority that is drawn from your observations in meetings, written documents of the religious group, interviews with congregational members, and other scholarly discussions of the group, the conclusion will be much more convincing than if it is based on only one or two of these types of data.

HOW TO PROCEED

Writing is a highly individual process. Some people can sit down and turn out an entire draft in a few hours; others will take days to sort through and set down ten pages. While some people prefer to write out a draft without attending to details, others cannot write unless they feel that each paragraph is ready to be put into the final version of the report.

Whatever your personal writing style, we strongly suggest that you try to write out a complete draft before worrying too much about perfecting each section or paragraph. Fill out each part of the outline, using the information from your notes to clarify each point. Err on the side of including more information and examples; it is always easier to cut material out later than it is to find examples to add. As you write each section, think about what you have already said, and how your present section can move you along to the next part of the paper.

12
Writing Style

Whatever else may be said about writing, the key advice is the most obvious: Always write clearly and directly. The purpose of writing is not to impress people with how intelligent you are, but to interest them in what you have to say and to convince them that what you have to say is correct. Don't use fancy terms unless they help you express what you want to say. Write simply and without any pretense; use the first person singular and the past tense (for example, "I attended two meetings") in describing your own experiences and feelings.

We cannot give you a lesson in grammar or spelling, but we include here a few of the most important rules for writing research papers. Add your own writing hints to this list, and use it as a checklist in both writing and editing your paper:

1. USE THE ACTIVE RATHER THAN THE PASSIVE VOICE WHENEVER POSSIBLE. (This is a clearer rule than one that reads: "The active rather than the passive voice should be used whenever possible.") Say: "He told me," not "I was told."

2. DON'T USE FOUR WORDS WHEN TWO WILL DO. ("The church was large and beautiful," not "The beautiful and stunning church was attractive and lovely.")

3. EACH PARAGRAPH SHOULD MAKE ONE POINT AND SUPPORT OR ELABORATE THAT ONE POINT. Seldom should paragraphs be more than half a page long.

4. AVOID RUN-ON SENTENCES. THEY USUALLY REFLECT RUN-ON THOUGHTS. Make your sentences as simple as possible. However, don't err in the other direction so far that your entire paper consists of nothing but short subject-verb-object sentences.

5. TRY TO VARY THE LENGTHS OF YOUR SENTENCES. Although simple sentences (subject-verb-object) are generally preferable, they can become tedious. Learn to use subordinate clauses, compound and complex sentences as well, and your writing will flow much more easily.

6. AVOID SENTENCE FRAGMENTS. Make sure you have a subject and a verb in each sentence. Don't experiment with "stream-of-consciousness" writing in a research paper.

7. USE A GOOD DICTIONARY OR WRITING GUIDE TO CHECK ANY SPELLING OR USAGE QUESTIONS YOU MAY HAVE. In addition to the ones already mentioned, a few particularly troubling (and recurring) examples are noted here:[1]

- *Among* refers to more than two, *between* to only two.
- Collective nouns take the plural verb only when the focus is on the various elements within each noun: "The trio were taking their seats." In most situations, use a singular verb: "The community was worshipping together."
- *In* refers to a present location, *into* refers to movement: "I sat in the pew," "We walked into the room."
- *Majority* always refers to more than 50 percent of the population, as does the term *most*. *Plurality* is a term referring to the largest single group, even if they are less than 50 percent of the total. For example, if you are comparing denominations, Roman Catholics constitute a plurality of American Christians, because they are the largest single denomination; they are not the majority, however, because there are more Protestants (of differing groups) than Roman Catholics.
- *Their* is a plural possessive; *there* points to location or a state of existence.

[1] Most of these examples are adapted from Barbara Lenmark-Ellis's very helpful book *How to Write Themes and Term Papers*, 2nd ed. (N.Y.: Barron's, 1981).

• *Who* is used to refer to people, *which* or *that* to refer to everything else: "The people, who had arrived on time, opened their prayer books." "The building, which was ornate and immense, was filled by ten o'clock." "The service that I attended was very crowded."

8. COLONS SHOULD BE USED PRIMARILY BEFORE A SERIES OR LISTING OF SOME SORT, OR BEFORE A QUOTATION.   For example: "The service consisted of three parts: silent meditation, a brief sermon, and a set of readings from the holy book." Semicolons are basically strong commas, and are used primarily when independent clauses are joined together in a single sentence; this should not be done too often, however, and even this sentence you are now reading should have been divided up. Semicolons are somewhat hazardous, because they allow you to avoid writing brief and clear sentences, so use them sparingly.

9. AVOID WORDS SUCH AS *really, quite*, OR *somewhat*.   They *really* add vagueness and *quite* diminish clarity.

10. BE CAREFUL TO SPECIFY THE ANTECEDENT REFERENT FOR ALL PRONOUNS.   If you begin a sentence with the phrase "This is the most important aspect . . .," be sure that the reader is perfectly clear about what *this* refers to.

11. OMIT MOST PARENTHETICAL OR QUALIFYING PHRASES FROM YOUR WRITING.   "I think," "It seems to me that," "It is often the case that"— such phrases are unnecessary most of the time.

12. USE THE FOLLOWING TERMS SPARINGLY AND APPROPRIATELY:

• *But*

• *However*

• *Nevertheless*

But begins a sentence or a phrase and is not followed by a comma; it should be used only to draw a clear contrast with a point that has just been made. ("Christians believe that Jesus Christ is the Messiah, but Jews do not." "Many religious services involve structured prayers and hymns. But Quaker meetings are usually much less structured.")

However begins a sentence and is followed by a comma. It is a somewhat weaker form of *but*. ("I wanted to take notes during the service. However, I was told that this was not allowed.")

Nevertheless is used the same way as *however* but is less appropriate for most situations.

13. KEEP YOUR ADJECTIVES AND ADVERBS AS CLOSE AS POSSIBLE TO THE WORDS THEY ARE MODIFYING. Dangling modifiers can result in some rather odd meanings: "Muslim services include bowing to Mecca, which take place one a day." Mecca does not take place once a day; the services do. In addition, don't string adjectives or adverbs together; two is a reasonable limit for most situations.

14. AVOID CLICHES, which are particularly well worn and overly familiar phrases and expressions. Some examples to stay away from at all costs: "Better late than never," "Ignorance is bliss," "Blue as the sky," "Thunderous applause."

15. REMEMBER THE PROPER USAGE OF *it's* AND *its*. *It's* is a contraction of *it is* and should be avoided in your writing. *Its* is the possessive form, such as in the sentence: "Its purpose is to provide a focus for worship." Notice that, although it is a possessive, *its* does not have an apostrophe.

16. GET RID OF REDUNDANT AND OVERWRITTEN EXPRESSIONS. For example, the phrase "a quiet silence" simply uses two words to say what one word expresses perfectly well. Similarly, don't say "These are the people who"; "These people" will do.

17. BRACKETS ([ ]) SHOULD BE USED VERY SPARINGLY IN YOUR PAPERS. There are only two appropriate situations in which to use brackets:

- If you need to include a parenthetical phrase within an already existing parenthetical phrase, such as in a bibliographical reference: "(Harvard University Press, 1989 [first published in 1968])." If you have such a phrase in your own text, rewrite the sentence rather than cramming parentheses within parentheses. For example, don't say this: "The monks were meditating (during the evening hours [only after they had eaten dinner])." Rewrite it: "After they had eaten, the monks meditated in the evening."
- If you want to indicate that something in a quotation is the way you found it in the original. This technique is often necessary to prevent yourself from looking as if you have made a typographical error. For instance, if you found a reference in a book on the "Judaic" way of prayer, and you know that "Jewish" is a far preferable term, you can include the term "Judaic" in a quotation but then put "[sic]" (meaning "thus") immediately after the term, so that your instructor will know that you are aware that this is not the best term, and that you have copied it down as it was written.

18. PUT PUNCTUATION MARKS AFTER PARENTHESES, AND NEVER INSIDE THE PARENTHESES UNLESS THEY ARE PART OF THE PARENTHETICAL REMARK ITSELF. For example: "They bowed down (or tried to), after finishing the silent prayer." "The service ended with a hymn. (The words are reprinted in the appendix to this report.)"

19. DASHES SHOULD BE USED ONLY TO SET OFF A PARTICULAR PHRASE OR WORD. "The congregation stood up—in unison—as the music began." Always use two or three hyphens for the dash, not just one. The single (a hyphen) is used to combine words.

20. USE ELLIPSES (. . .) WHEN YOU ARE OMITTING A SECTION FROM A DIRECT QUOTATION, such as in quoting from an interview: "I have belonged to this church for several years . . . ever since my cousin brought me here as a young man." Be careful not to cut and paste quotations in such a way as to distort the meaning, however.

21. COMMAS ARE COMPLICATED BUT ESSENTIAL FOR GOOD WRITING. The situations in which commas are necessary include the following:

- Lists of items: "The people were given prayer shawls, small hats, and prayer books to take with them into the service."

- Separating clauses: "When the people stood up, the Rabbi opened the Ark." "The Bible is the Word of God, according to the people I talked to."

- Before short quotations: "The person next to me said, 'Don't write anything down during the service.'"

22. THE "VOICE" YOU WRITE IN DEPENDS ON THE TYPE OF PAPER AND THE TOPIC. Whether you use the first person or the third person, the most important point is to focus the reader's attention on the content of the paper. In discussing the history of a religious group, for example, avoid giving the reader the impression of looking over your shoulder. Don't use phrases such as: "I was surprised to learn that . . . ," "I was told that . . . ," "My impression in reading this book was that . . . ." Simply describe what you learned, what people said, and what happened.

However, if you are describing your own observations or interviews, there may be times when the first person singular is the most appropriate voice to use. The reader is probably interested not just in what you saw, but in how you felt and what you did during the observation. Because these pieces of information are themselves the "data" of interest, you can talk about them in the first person. Similarly, if you are describing a conversation with someone else, it is perfectly appropriate to say , "I asked him about his beliefs regarding the Trinity, and he replied that . . . ."

Avoid use of the first person plural, expecially when making global assessments of broad generalizations. For example, the following sorts of phrases usually put readers off: "We can conclude that . . . ," "We have recognized by now that . . . ," "Our opinions are that . . . ." If you find yourself using such phrases in your draft, ask yourself what you are trying to say, and recast the sentence to indicate either that you are expressing a personal opinion or that something is a matter of common knowledge. If the former, use the first person singular; if the latter, just make the statement.

23. Avoid any language that is oriented toward a particular gender.   The words *he* and *his* refer to men, *not* to human beings in general and should not be used to refer to all of humanity. This is a matter of some dispute in contemporary American society, and your instructor may have some guidance to provide for your papers. As a general rule, we suggest trying to recast sentences to avoid having to use odd syntax such as "he/she," "he or she," or other ill-sounding terms. If you need to, however, "he or she" is far preferable to other unpronounceable alternatives.

Here are a few hints that should help you write in a more gender-neutral manner:[2]

- Rewrite sentences to avoid male references, unless you are referring to a specific male person. For example, change: "When saying his prayers, the Christian tries to think about his relationship to Jesus," to the following: 'When praying, Christians try to think about how they are related to Jesus." Instead of: "A minister will use his voice to make an impression," try: "Ministers use their voices to make an impression." (If only males may function as ministers in your group, you may use the male pronoun, but include a footnote early in the paper to explain your usage.)

- Avoid *the men* as a subject or object, unless all the people are males—try *they* or *the people*.

- Change words to focus on *human* rather than *man* wherever possible: *Mankind* should be *humanity* or *people*, for example; *man-made* should be changed to *manufactured* or *made; wise men* should be *wise people*.

- Avoid stereotyped expressions that include male language: "The right man for the job" can be altered to "the right person for the job"; "mothering" can be changed to "parenting" or "nurturing."

- Watch out for writing in ways that reinforce conventional views of the roles of men and women. For example: *man and wife* should be changed to *husband and wife* or *man and woman; housewife* should be *homemaker* or *consumer*, unless you are dealing with a culture in which women are always the only ones who stay home; *woman minister* should be changed to *minister*, unless you are describing a particular person and noting gender as a significant part of your description.

24. Be cautious in underlining words to show emphasis.   Ideally, the structure and syntax should provide sufficient emphasis without having to rely on underlining. (Avoid sentences such as the following: "One of the most <u>common</u> mistakes is to rely <u>too</u> heavily on <u>underlining</u> . . . .") Experiment with reorganizing a paragraph to give more emphasis to a particular point, or find ways to underscore the important themes by devoting a subsection to them.

---

[2] We are indebted to Prentice Hall for many of the following examples.

25. WHEN A SENTENCE BEGINS WITH A NUMBER, YOU MUST SPELL IT OUT; IN ALL OTHER CASES, YOU CAN USE THE ARABIC CHARACTERS.   For example: "Fifty people were present at the service; 30 were women, 10 were men, and 10 were very young children."

26. IN REFERRRING TO DATES, CONTEXT DETERMINES WHETHER YOU NEED TO ADD "A.D." (MEANING *anno Domini*," IN THE YEAR OF THE LORD) OR "B.C."(BEFORE CHRIST).   If you wish, and particularly if you are dealing with Jewish material, you can substitute "C.E." (of the common era) and "B.C.E." (before the common era). Always include the B.C. or B.C.E. when it applies. On the other hand, if all of your examples are drawn from the last century or so, you do not need to put any such notation after the date (1840 is fine, for example). But if you are referring to any events occurring before 500 A.D., it is often clearer to add the notation. The best rule to follow is: If there is the chance of confusion, include the notation after the date; otherwise, leave it out.

Commas are not put in dates, except for dates of more than four figures: 1200 B.C., but 22,000 B.C.

27. WHEN YOU TYPE YOUR PAPER, REMEMBER TO DIVIDE WORDS AT THE END OF A LINE AT THE PROPER PLACE.   The general rule is to divide words at the end of each pronounced syllable; consult a dictionary if you are unsure. Use a hyphen at the end of the line, and do not put an additional hyphen at the beginning of the next line. Never divide words in such a way as to create only one letter on either side (e.g., e-nough), and never divide a past-tense verb to leave the "-ed" alone on the next line (e.g., pass-ed).

28. AVOID EXCLAMATION POINTS, EXCEPT WHERE THEY APPEAR IN QUO-TATIONS, REFER TO AN OUTCRY SOMEONE HAS MADE, OR ARE USED TO MAKE AN IRONIC OR SARCASTIC COMMENT.   The overuse of the exclamation point to emphasize or underscore a point is legion! Professors are sick of it! So don't do it! Instead, rewrite the sentence to increase its power, change its location to give it more prominence, or (in very rare cases) underline the relevant word or phrase.

When in doubt on any questions of grammar or spelling, use a standard style guide such as the *MLA Style Manual,* the *Publication Manual of the American Psychological Association, A Manual for Writers* by Kate L. Turabian, or another book suggested by your instructor.

13

Documenting
Your Sources

AVOIDING PLAGIARISM

Learning how to document your sources is important for two reasons. First, the reader needs to know where you have gathered your information, on what information your conclusions are based, and how extensively you have read concerning your topic. Second, you may be guilty of plagiarism if you have not adequately indicated precisely which parts of your paper are not your own. Since plagiarism is an extremely serious offense, it is important to learn how to avoid it by citing your sources in appropriate ways.

As a general rule, any information that is either commonly known or constitutes your own opinions or perceptions does not need documentation. For example, the occurrence and dates of well-known historical events, the most essential beliefs of religious groups, and the central terms used in community meetings or services do not need to be footnoted. If you find the same set of facts or interpretations in several sources, you are fairly safe in assuming that you do not need to footnote the references. If, on the other hand, you find conflicting views of this information, you should give an example of at least one source on each side of the argument, if only to inform the reader that the disagreement is not something you have invented on your own.

Paraphrasing is a good alternative to filling your paper with direct quotations, but you must be very careful with how you paraphrase. You cannot simply change an occasional word, or shift around sentences or phrases, or use the identical structure or content in repeating what someone else has said. A valid paraphrase is not just something said in your own words but something which, while indebted to someone else, represents your own writing.

If you have a paragraph that constitutes a summary of what someone else has said, you must document this fact, even though none of that author's words were used. If the entire paragraph represents a summary of one author's thoughts, place a footnote at the end of the paragraph. If individual sentences reflect the views of different authors, it is better to footnote each sentence separately. However, you can place a composite footnote at the end of the paragraph, in which you list each source in order of appearance in the paragraph.

In addition, you cannot refer to a source you have not consulted yourself, unless you make it perfectly clear that the reference comes from someone else. For example, if you are referring to John Calvin's interpretation of a passage from Saint Augustine, you cannot footnote or discuss the Augustine passage directly if you have not read it yourself. Instead, your text should make it clear that you are saying what Calvin has said, and the footnote should repeat that fact (e.g., "1. Augustine, *The Trinity*: referred to in John Calvin's *The Institutes of the Christian Religion* . . ."). Trying to make it appear that you have read more than you have is a serious violation of research ethics.

The best way to avoid plagiarism is to be careful and systematic throughout the research process. Take careful notes, writing down all relevant bibliographic information and being sure to distinguish between direct quotations and your own summaries. Use direct quotations sparingly, but make sure that your paraphrases are in your own words. If you find that you cannot paraphrase something very easily, then include it as a footnoted direct quote. Finally, proofread your paper carefully, and ask yourself whether you might inadvertently have used someone else's words or ideas as your own.

If you are ever in doubt whether you need to document a particular point, either ask your instructor, or err on the side of footnoting the section. It is far better to have a paper marked down for too much documentation than to be disciplined severely for plagiarism. Remember that documenting your sources is an issue of moral character, not merely one of literary style. Ignorance of the rules is unlikely to be an adequate excuse.

QUOTATIONS

You will probably have various types of quotations in your research paper. If you have interviewed people in a religious group, you will have specific comments that they made, either in taped transcripts or in your own handwritten notes. If you attended a service, you will have some specific prayers or meditations drawn from the formal service, perhaps copied down after the service from a prayer book. In addition, you should have notes from books or articles you may have consulted, as well as relevant comments made by your professor in class or even by some of your fellow students in discussions with them about your project.

How do you use these quotations? In most situations, these comments and writings will form the basis of your evidence and therefore will serve as the underlying reference for most of the paper. But when, if ever, should you quote *directly* from what other people have said? There are three general rules for deciding how and when to refer to them:

1. **Use a direct quotation only when it helps you make a point or give an example.** Never quote simply to prove that you have taken notes or copied something down.

2. **Keep direct quotations short.** Readers become bored and bogged down by long quotations. As a general rule, never use a quotation that is more than ten lines long (single-spaced), and try to keep them under seven lines. Paraphrase wherever possible.

3. **Use direct quotations sparingly.** Although there are exceptions, you should not have more than one or two extended (more than three lines) quotations on any page of text.

When you use a quotation, integrate it into the rest of the text. The sentence preceding it should indicate both where it came from and why it is significant (for example: "As the minister said about the importance of reading the Bible during the service: . . ."). The first sentence or two after the quotation should interpret the significance of the passage and state your own conclusions about its meaning. (For example: "This comment reflects the belief of this group that the Bible is not merely an important book but the source of divine authority.")

If you force yourself to write these preceding and following sentences, you will often find that you don't need the quotation at all. In that case, take it out and just summarize the point yourself. Only include the quotation when you think it is necessary to support your conclusion or when the way in which the point is expressed is particularly interesting or revealing.

You may be nervous about stating other writers' observations in your own words. However, you must learn to do this, or else your entire paper will consist of a string of quotations. Your task in organizing and analyzing the data is to decide what is important, develop the appropriate way to say it, and then present the evidence in a clear and systematic way. The main voice in the paper should be your own, not that of one or two of your informants.

The proper form for quoting is as follows:

FORM FOR QUOTING SHORT QUOTATIONS

Donald Martin wrote: "Only a fool would believe that one religion is intrinsically better than another."

This would be followed by a footnote, of course. Note that the quotation is integrated into the text, and that the quotation marks follow the closing period. Periods and commas are always placed within the closing quotation marks, while other punctuation marks occur outside the quotation marks, unless they are present in the original quotation.

FORM FOR LONGER QUOTATIONS

As Donald Martin has written:

Only a fool would believe that one religion is intrinsically better than another. The appropriate question to ask is not whether one religion is better but whether and how it is able to meet the needs of the culture in which it has developed. [single-space quote]

Martin's point is particularly applicable to this study of the role of Buddhism in the United States.

Note that no quotation marks are used in such situations, and that the entire passage is both single-spaced and indented from the left-hand side of the page. The sentence before the quotation serves as a lead-in, and the sentence following it either interprets the quote or provides a bridge between it and the next part of the paper. Again, a footnote would be placed at the end of the quotation.

Brackets ([]) are used in quotations for two purposes. First, if something in the quotation is clearly incorrect, you should indicate to the reader that you are aware of that fact. Remember that all direct quotations *must* be written precisely the way they appear in the source from which you are quoting. To indicate the problem, you can put the word [*sic*] in the quotation immediately following the mistake. For example: "Humperdinck wrote: 'Opra [sic] is incredibly boring.'"

Second, brackets are useful for including a parenthetical comment of your own in the middle of a quotation. This practice should be used very sparingly, because it tends to dilute the force of the quotation and distract the reader's attention. But there are situations in which it might be useful, such as in the following case: "The minister said: 'My congregation meets [for prayer services] every evening.'"

In this example, the minister actually said, "My congregation meets every evening," but it is important for the reader to know that this involves prayer services. To indicate this fact, the writer of the paper includes the parenthetical comment within the quotation and puts it in brackets. Once again, use this technique only when necessary.

Quotations from religious books occasionally take different forms. For most books, use the standard form. In the case of the Bible, you do not need to use a full citation. Simply put the name of the particular book of the Bible in parentheses after the quotation or reference, followed by the chapter and verse (or verses) cited. Abbreviations for the names of the books can be found in the front of the Bible. For example: Matt. 7:1-4 (referring to Matthew, chapter 7, verses 1–4); Lev. 20:3 (referring to Leviticus, chapter 20, verse 3).

Unless you are referring to the King James Bible, indicate which translation you are using the first time you cite a biblical passage (e.g., Revised Standard Version or the Jerusalem Bible). If you are going to be citing the Bible more than once or twice, ask your instructor which translation is preferred; your library should have copies of the most common ones.

FOOTNOTES

Footnotes are essential in informing the reader of the source of either a quotation or a summarized point. If you have paraphrased someone or referred to something they said to you, a footnote will make it clear to the reader that the content of the point is drawn from another source. The same footnote form should be used whether you are quoting directly or paraphrasing from someone else. Remember, however, that simply footnoting a passage of your own prose is not sufficient if you are in fact quoting directly from the source; in such cases, you must use quotation marks, or indent and single-space longer quotations, as just discussed.

There are various forms of footnoting, and we will suggest one of the most commonly used versions here. (As always, if your instructor has given you a different set of guidelines for footnote style, follow those directions.) A raised number should be placed above the final punctuation mark in the sentence containing the reference; the numbers simply proceed sequentially throughout the paper (do not start over at "1" in each new section of the report). The footnote reference itself is then either placed at the very bottom of the page, or it is placed together with all other footnotes at the end of the paper. (We recommend placing footnotes at the bottom of the page if this is easily done either on computer or by a good typist; if this is difficult, place them at the end of the paper.)

Each footnote begins with the raised footnote number and should then take the following style, depending on what sort of source you are referring to.

FORM FOR CITING A BOOK

Author(s), *Title* (Place of Publication: Publisher, Date of Publication), page number(s).

Examples:

Samuel Smith, *Religious Views of the Smith Family* (Smithville, Ohio: Smith Publishing Company, 1989), p. 3.

Samuel Smith and Edwina Smith, *How the Smith Family Prayed*, ed. by Henrietta Smith (Smithville, Ohio: Smith Publishing Company, 1989), pp. 65–68.

FORM FOR CITING A JOURNAL ARTICLE

Author(s), "Title," *Name of Journal* Volume # (Date of Publication): page number(s).

Example:

John Smith and Sally Smythe, "Smiths and Smythes in Religious Conflict," *Journal of Religious History* 10 (Sept, 1989):33.

FORM FOR CITING AN ARTICLE
IN AN ANTHOLOGY OR EDITED COLLECTION

Joseph Smith, "My Life as a Mormon," in *Religious Experiences in America*. ed. Samuel Smith (New York: Regular Publishers, 1989), pp. 5–6.

FORM FOR CITING AN INTERVIEW

Name of interviewee, nature of contact, date of contact.

Example:

Abigail Smith, personal interview, Jan. 4, 1989.

FORM FOR CITING ENCYCLOPEDIA ARTICLES

Encyclopedia Britannica, 12th ed. (1944), s.v. "Buddhism," by Mortimer Smith.

["s.v." stands for "sub verbo," meaning "under the word," and is used to indicate the subject reference where the article can be found.]

FORM FOR CITING NEWSPAPER ARTICLES

"Those Amazing Believers," *Los Angeles Times*, 14 March 1988, sec. 3, p. C12.

[The "sec." refers to the section of the paper, if it is labeled.]

Footnotes to the Bible need include only the book, chapter, and verse (e.g., Matt. 5:14–15). If a version other than the King James is being used, put its name in parenthesis at the end of the first footnote referring to that translation—for example: I Samuel 4:20 (Revised Standard Version).

If the book or article is translated, and the translator is listed at the front, include the name in the footnote immediately following the title, such as: St. Augustine, *The Trinity*, trans. Roberto Trio (Austin, Texas: University of Texas Press, 1972), p. 201.

Note all later editions following the title (this does not refer to reprintings, which constitute the same text as the original printing); later editions will always be noted either on the title page or on the copyright page. Reference them as follows: Jimmy Carter, *My Life as a Baptist*, 2nd ed. (Atlanta, Georgia: Amazing Press, 1988), p. 44.

If you make more than one reference to a particular source, you may shorten the reference, simply referring to the last name of the author (if there is only one book or article by that author) and including the relevant page number(s) for this reference. If there are several different sources by the same author, also include a shortened version of the title of the article or book.

Alternatively, you can use the term *ibid.* (meaning "in the same place") for consecutive references to the same source. Be careful in using this form, however, because any intervening footnotes will confuse the reader and leave your references unintelligible. For example, the following is a correct way to footnote two consecutive references to Tunney's book:

CITING SAME SOURCE MORE THAN ONCE

1. Gene Tunney, *Boxing My Way to Faith* (Los Angeles: The Gym Press, 1940), p. 38.

2. Ibid., p. 42.

If there had been an intervening footnote to another source, however, *ibid.* could not be used. To be on the safe side, we suggest that you avoid *ibid.* entirely, and simply use the author's name, remembering to include a short part of the title if you are referring to more than one article or book by the same author.

You can also use footnotes to make substantive comments on your own text, when you are afraid that putting them in the body of the paper will distract the reader. Don't do this very often, however; in most cases, it is far preferable to rewrite the paragraph to make the point in the text, or include it in a brief parenthetical comment at the end of the paragraph. Use substantive footnotes only when you are commenting on something from the standpoint of the writer, not when you are developing a point further.

For example, you might be quoting from the Bible, and you want to tell the reader which version you are referring to. A purely referential footnote would simply list the Bible used, for example, "Revised Standard Version." But you might want to tell the reader why you have chosen this version, particularly if you are going to be quoting from other passages later on in the paper. If this is an important point, it should appear in the body of the paper; if it is irrelevant, leave it out completely; if it is something of interest but it is not particularly crucial, you can include it in a brief substantive footnote, perhaps following the first time you cite such a passage. For example, if the passage of text ended with the quotation itself and a numbered footnote ("1"), such a footnote might read as follows:

---

1. Matt. 5:10 (RSV). I have used this translation because of its reputed accuracy, and because it is the one most often quoted from in the sources I have used in this paper.

If you find that you have more than three or four substantive footnotes in your entire paper, go back and ask whether you need to include these points at all, and, if so, whether you can put them in the text. In making such decisions, remember that you are trying to find a balance between a paper that flows smoothly from one point to the next, and a paper that includes enough information to support your arguments and conclusions. The two goals may not always overlap, and much of your work as a writer will lie in learning to make the correct judgments.

BIBLIOGRAPHY (OR SOURCES CITED)

Your professor may require a list of all the sources you have used in preparing the paper. Such a list is often termed a "bibliography," but the broader term "sources" allows you to include interviews and other unwritten types of information. If there are any other sources you have used, in addition to the ones you cited in your footnotes, you should include them here. This list can include a list of people you interviewed if there are only two or three people; alternatively, you can provide a separate list of interviews (organized by date) in an appendix immediately before this section.

Your bibliography section should be organized in alphabetical order, using the last name of the author (or the title of the source if there is no author). Do not number the entries themselves.

The following form is an appropriate one for such entries:

FORM FOR CITING A BOOK IN A BIBLIOGRAPHY

Author(s). *Title*. Place of publication: Publisher, Date of Publication.

Example:

Smith, Samuel. *Religious Views of the Smith Family*. Smithville, Ohio: Smith Publishing Co., 1989.

FORM FOR CITING AN ARTICLE IN A BIBLIOGRAPHY

Author(s). "Title." *Name of Journal* Volume Number (Date): page number(s).

Example:

Smith, John, and Smythe, Sally. "Smiths and Smythes in Religious Conflict." *Journal of Religious History* 10 (Sept. 1989):25–38.

If you have conducted interviews, you can either include them in the bibliography or list them separately in an appendix appearing just before this section. In either event, the form is very simple:

FORM FOR CITING AN INTERVIEW IN A BIBLIOGRAPHY

Caesar, Julius. Personal Interview. March 15, 44 B.C.

If you have any specific questions about footnote or source citation style, consult a manual such as *The Chicago Manual of Style* or Kate Turabian's *Student's Guide for Writing College Papers*, both of which can probably be found in your library or bookstore.

If you have any questions about the appropriate style to use for footnoting, ask your instructor. This is particularly important because of the danger of being accused of plagiarism. It is better to ask an obvious question than to assume that you are footnoting correctly and find out later that you were wrong.

The handling of quotations from interviews is particularly important. Include verbatim statements from any interviews you may have performed, since this will allow the reader to develop a better sense of how people expressed themselves and their beliefs and attitudes. Use the actual names of the people you spoke with *only* if you have received their permission to do so; otherwise, make up names for each person, or refer to them in more general terms (for example: "A member of the Vestry said . . .") Make certain that in your methods section you describe how you have dealt with the issue of confidentiality.

14

Formatting and Editing Your Paper

The final draft of the paper should follow this organizational format:

- Title Page
- Table of Contents
- Introduction
- Sections of the Paper
- Conclusion
- Footnotes (if listed at end of paper)
- Appendices (if any)
- Bibliography or Sources Cited (if required)

TITLE PAGE

The title page should include the following pieces of information: the title of the paper, your name, the name (and course number, if there is one) of the course, the name of the instructor, and the date on which the paper is being submitted. If you wish, you may include the name of the college or university as well.

The form is somewhat flexible, but we would suggest the following. Center the title between left and right margins, leaving about ten or twelve lines at the top of the page. Put your name directly underneath. Put the information about the course, instructor, and date in the lower left-hand corner, leaving approximately six lines at the bottom.

Here is an example of a title page following this format:

```
            PRAYER AND MEDITATION IN A QUAKER SERVICE:

            AN EXAMPLE OF STRUCTURED SILENCE




                            Your Name










Religion 201a

Introduction to Religion

Professor George Fox


May 3, 1992
```

Keep your title simple. The example above includes a subtitle, which provides a bit more information about the theme of the paper. Subtitles are not required, however.

The title page, of course, is the first page of the paper. If you are binding the paper in a folder of some sort, put a label on the cover of the folder with the same information that appears on the title page, so the instructor does not have to open up the folder to see what is in it.

Do not type anything on the other side of the title page, or on the other side of *any* pages of your paper. The title page has no page number and is not counted as page 1 in numbering the paper.

TABLE OF CONTENTS

The second page of the paper should be the table of contents, which is designed to tell the reader precisely how the paper is organized and where each topic and section will be found. Simply list all the sections of your paper, and list the page on which each section (or subsection) begins. This means, of course, that you will be typing this page last, in order to determine the page numbers correctly. Include a listing of everything that follows the table of contents, including the introduction, appendices, and bibliography or footnote lists. The table of contents is not numbered and does not count when you begin to number the pages of your paper.

An example of the proper form for a table of contents follows:

HEADINGS AND SUBHEADINGS

Your paper will be much more readable if you provide section titles informing the reader of the topic you are now going to discuss. Including headings and subheadings also allows you to make sure that you have a clear organizational direction for your paper.

The headings should be the same brief phrases you would use in an outline of your paper. For example, notice the heading of this section: "Headings and Subheadings." Everything discussed until the appearance of the next heading (or the next new chapter) should deal with that topic. Headings should be brief but informative, providing enough information so the reader knows what is being discussed.

If you have long sections, you may want to use subheadings as well. Be consistent in the way you format each "level" of your headings. For example, here is the style we have used in this book:

First level: Chapter titles (centered, all words capitalized, bold type)

Second level: Section headings (flush with left margin, capitalized, bold type)

Third level: Subsection headings (indented five spaces from margin, first letter only capitalized, bold type)

The resulting text looks like this:

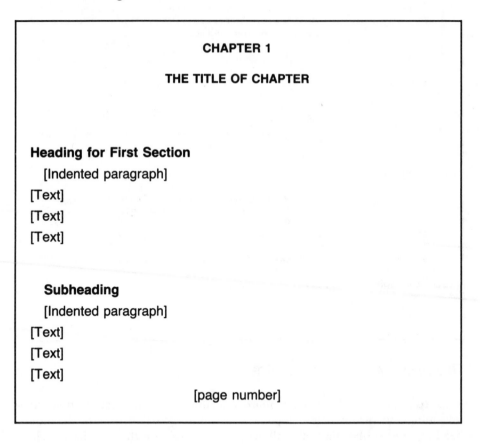

CHAPTER 1

THE TITLE OF CHAPTER

Heading for First Section
   [Indented paragraph]
[Text]
[Text]
[Text]

   Subheading
   [Indented paragraph]
[Text]
[Text]
[Text]

[page number]

You may choose a different style if you wish, but remember to follow it throughout your paper. You should not use headings if you have only one heading topic for a chapter; also, don't use subheadings if there is only one subheading section within a larger heading section.

Once you have completed the draft, include all headings and subheadings in your table of contents draft. You might decide to leave them out of the table of contents in your final draft, but it is extremely useful to make a detailed outline, to make sure that you have followed an intelligible and consistent format. Remember that the point of including headings and subheadings is to make the paper easier to follow; if they don't serve that purpose, redo them.

INTRODUCTION TO THE PAPER

The introductory section should be the last section you write (except for the table of contents). After all, since the purpose of the introduction is to tell the reader what the paper will include, you can hardly know this in detail until you have completed your draft.

The opening paragraph of your paper should answer four questions:

1. What is your topic?
2. Why is it worth writing about?
3. What research methods did you use?
4. How is the paper organized?

You do not need to answer each question in this order or have a separate sentence responding to each question. But by the time the reader has completed the first page, he or she should have a good idea of the answers to all four questions.

One of the best ways to begin a paper is to tell your audience why and how you became interested in your topic. Don't make something up, but just try to explain why you thought this was an interesting subject. (Of course, if you don't think it is worth writing about, you should choose another topic.) There are many reasons why people find different subjects interesting; all the reasons are valid. For example, you might have had a childhood experience with a particular religious tradition, and you have always wondered what it would have been like to be a member of that group. Or your best friend might pray every morning, and you could never figure out why he did that and what that meant to him. Or you could have read an article in a magazine about a religious movement that practiced some odd rituals, and you were curious about the meaning of these practices.

The introduction should tell the reader just enough about the topic so that the rest of the paper makes sense. You should not give any details about the topic, or even give your conclusion. If you have a specific question or hypothesis, state it briefly here.

Finally, give a very brief outline of the remainder of the paper, including a sentence or two about the methodology you used to research and write the paper. The outline should merely touch upon the overall flow of the paper, rather than give information about the contents of each section.

Here is a sample introduction:

Human communities often struggle with problems of leadership. In religious settings, the leaders are particularly important, especially in traditions where the leader is perceived as representing the will and interpreting the word of God to the members. In this paper, I will examine the role of the leader in an American Buddhist community.

Buddhism is a particularly interesting religion to study in this regard. As a religion that has been imported to the United States, it can be expected to take on some of the characteristics of other American religious groups. At the same time, its "foreign" origins would be expected to reveal some interesting differences and tensions. Because I have been raised in a Protestant Christian community, I was interested in discovering whether the leaders of Buddhist communities play roles similar to those of the ministers in my church.

The paper is based on several visits to a Buddhist community, interviews with leaders and members, and several articles I read about Buddhism in America. In addition, I have discussed the issues with a minister in my own religious community and have drawn some comparisons wherever possible.

I will begin with a brief discussion of the group itself, including some background about its roots in Japan and the nature of its membership in the United States. Next, I will focus on the role of the leader in the group, using my observations and interviews to develop a model of how the leader functions. Some interpretations and conclusions follow these sections, leading to some opinions about the importance of leadership in religious communities in general.

Notice both the structure and the tone of this introduction. The topic is set in a broader context—namely, the importance of leadership and authority in human communities. In addition, the distinctive nature of Buddhist religious leadership is acknowledged and used as an enticement for reading the paper. The reader is left wondering precisely how Buddhists do organize themselves, and becomes curious about how that differs from how Protestants do so. The creation of this curiosity is a purpose of the introduction to any paper.

Let us assume that the research project is one that involves only library work, rather than empirical observation. The following sort of introduction might then be used:

What happens to a religious community that is opposed to sexual activity? Although many religious traditions have made room for celibacy within the ranks of their members, few have taken a principled position against sex and reproduction. What would be the result if this did occur?

I will examine one group that did, in fact, adopt precisely such a position--namely, the Shaker community in the United States. I will focus on the following two questions: (1) Why did the Shakers adopt this view toward sex? (2) What have been the major consequences of such a position, from the standpoint of the continued growth and survival of the community?

The report is based upon several books and articles providing historical information about the Shakers, as well as some documentary accounts written by members and observers. After briefly discussing the history of the group, I will consider the theological reasons for the group's attitude toward sex and will then examine the various tensions and conflicts that this view created. The final section considers the survival of the group in the future, and draws some conclusions about the place of celibacy in religious communities.

Notice again that the introduction does not provide details or specifics, but instead gives an overall look at the topic, its importance, and the direction the paper will take. The ability to define one or two specific questions to be addressed by the paper is extremely helpful, since this then serves as a focus for the reader's attention for the remainder of the report.

CONCLUSION OF THE PAPER

The concluding section of your paper does not need to be very long. If you have done your work well in organizing and developing your evidence and arguments in the rest of the paper, all that should be required is a brief summing up of the major point (or points), and a few sentences about the broader significance of what you have found.

The most common mistakes made in conclusions are of two varieties: repeating everything that has been said, and claiming too much from what has been said. The first problem usually stems from an insufficiently organized paper; if you are not sure what the major points are, you will have trouble locating them and placing them (and *only* them) in the conclusion. You can assume that the instructor has in fact read the entire paper already, so you don't need to repeat the entire process of reasoning or cite the evidence again. A brief one- or two- sentence summary of the major point or points is sufficient.

The second problem comes when the writer tries to draw grandiose conclusions from a fairly limited study. If you have just discovered that the Unification Church has a particular understanding of the significance of prayer, you cannot conclude that all (or even most) new religious movements have such a viewpoint, nor can you conclude that the Unification Church also has other distinctive beliefs or practices (unless you have already provided evidence for that in your paper). It is quite sufficient to conclude that you have found this particular thing to be true of this particular group, and to leave it at that. No one is expecting your paper to be the definitive discussion of a major theme.

In drawing broader conclusions, however, you can certainly feel free to speculate about the meaning or significance of what you have found, so long as you label the speculation as such. One useful technique is to begin the concluding section with a paragraph repeating the major point of the paper, and then to indicate clearly at the beginning of the next paragraph that you are now going to make some educated guesses about what this might mean. Feel free to let yourself go and come up with intriguing and offbeat ideas; remember, however, that the quality of these ideas will not offset a poorly written paper.

It is certainly appropriate to use humor or personal opinions and feelings at this point in the paper. (Indeed, it is fine to use them anywhere, but do so with caution. The body of the paper should be a serious and well-reasoned discussion, not a comedy routine or a personal confession.) Your instructor will usually appreciate your willingness to think about what you have learned from the project and how it might apply to other related issues or problems you are concerned with. And nothing is as gratifying to a teacher as to feel that a student is motivated to continue thinking, and even writing, about a topic that was first discovered in a particular course.

SPACING AND PAGE FORMAT

The paper should be double-spaced (except for extended quotations) and typed on only one side of each page. Margins should be approximately one inch on all four sides, although you should have a slightly wider margin on the left side if you are putting the paper in a binder or folder.

Direct quotations should be indented and single-spaced if they are more than three lines long. (If shorter, they should be included in the body of the text without indenting and should be enclosed in quotation marks.) Footnotes and bibliographies should also be single-spaced.

Number each page either at the top or the bottom of the page. Use Arabic numbers (e.g., 1, 2, 3) for all page numbers. The title page and table of contents page are not numbered; the first page of text is considered page 1. If you are numbering your pages at the top, put the page number at the bottom of any page with a centered section heading at the top of the page.

EDITING AND PROOFREADING

Editing (rewriting, redrafting) is probably the most commonly overlooked stage of paper writing. If you do not write the paper until the night before it is due, you obviously will not have time to edit, and your first draft will be your last. If the paper is going to reflect your best efforts, leave yourself at least three or four days to rewrite.

We recommend completing the entire first draft and then putting the paper aside for a day or two. Do something else during the intervening time; if you are aware of some obvious holes in the paper, you could conduct a bit more research if necessary, but don't reread the paper or your notes. This procedure allows you to gain some distance from the paper so that your rereading will be fresher.

When you finally sit down to rewrite, read through the paper carefully twice, with a different purpose in mind each time:

1. The first reading should focus *purely* on content and organization. Ask yourself the following questions as you read: Does the paper flow from point to point? Have I said everything I wanted to say? Is the major theme clearly expressed? Have I presented enough evidence to support each of my points? Are there any unnecessary sections? Keep a running tally of your reactions on a separate piece of paper, to refer back to later.

After you finish this first reading, go back and spend whatever time is necessary making the changes you have suggested to yourself. Don't be afraid to make radical changes; treat the first draft as a rough draft, not as a part of you that you can't bear to alter. Be ruthless when necessary, slashing out whole sections and eliminating (and adding) quotations and examples. If you need to tinker with the organization of the paper, do so without remorse.

If you have never carefully rewritten anything, you may be surprised to find how difficult it is. It is natural to become personally invested in something we write, and it is precisely for that reason that rewriting is so seldom done—and so important to do. Treat the paper as if you were reading someone else's product rather than your own. The more distance you can get from the fact that *you* have written the paper, the more thorough a job you will do of rewriting in a positive way.

When you have finished this stage of rewriting, perform the entire task again in exactly the same way, asking the same questions and taking notes again. Go back and rewrite one more time. Do this as many times as necessary, until you can read the paper and feel that "this is the best I can do." The more you rewrite, the better the paper will be. This sounds like a prescription for endless work, but it is in fact a guide for good writing.

2. You are now ready to read the paper through with your second agenda in mind. This time, pay attention *only* to questions of form and style. (Remember, this assumes that you have already perfected the paper in terms of content and theme.) Reread the section on style in this part of the book, and then read your draft slowly, asking yourself the following sorts of questions:

- Is this point clearly expressed?
- Is this the best word to use here?
- Is this phrase grammatically correct?
- Is this sentence too long?

Make corrections on the draft as you go along.

After you have performed your editing, type out the final draft of the paper, or print it out on your computer. Once you have done so, *proofread* the entire paper carefully, checking especially for typing mistakes and grammatical or spelling errors. If you have to make an occasional correction, you can make it on the paper with a good pen; if you have more than one or two such changes on any given page, retype or reprint the page. Regardless of how good the substance of your paper might be, no reader will enjoy reading it if it is marked up with multiple erasures and corrections.

After proofreading the paper yourself, consider asking a friend to read it over for you to check for errors in spelling or grammar. Otherwise, type out a title page, bind the paper (with either staples or a binder), and turn it in on time. Congratulations.

Appendix 1
Membership in Religious Organizations

The data included here illustrate the membership figures of most of the major religious groups in the United States. Such information should be interpreted cautiously, however, because data are usually self-reported, and groups differ in their definition of who counts as a member.

First, it is useful to examine membership figures in the United States as compared with worldwide membership statistics.

WORLDWIDE POPULATIONS OF THE MAJOR WORLD RELIGIONS
(in millions)

Christians	1,620.0
Muslims	840.23
Hindus	648.0
Buddhists	307.5
Jews	18.0
Shintoists	3.5
Confucians	5.65
Tribal	97.5
Chinese Folk Religion	203.0

| Others | 114.0 |
| Nonbelievers | 927.7 |

(From Denise and John Carmody, *The Story of World Religions* [Mountain View, CA: Mayfield Pub. Co., 1988], p. 9.)

The membership figures for major groups in the United States are as follows.

MEMBERSHIP IN MAJOR RELIGIOUS GROUPS IN THE UNITED STATES

Roman Catholic Church	53.0 million
Southern Baptist Convention	14.5 million
National Baptist Convention, U.S.A.	5.5 million
National Baptist Convention of America	2.7 million
American Baptist	1.7 million
Baptist Bible Fellowship	1.4 million
United Methodist Church	9.3 million
Lutheran Church in America	2.9 million
Lutheran Church, Missouri Synod	2.7 million
American Lutheran Church	2.3 million
Church of God in Christ	3.7 million
A.M.E.	2.2 million
A.M.E. Zion	1.2 million
Presbyterian Church, U.S.A.	3.0 million
Assemblies of God	2.1 million
United Pentecostal Church	500,000
Pentecostal Holiness Church	113,000
Pentecostal Church of God	90,000
Episcopal Church	2.7 million
United Church of Christ	1.7 million

Christian Church and Churches of Christ .... 1.1 million

Christian Church (Disciples of Christ) .... 1.1 million

Jehovah's Witnesses 730,000

Seventh Day Adventists 650,000

Greek Orthodox Church .... 2.0 million
Orthodox Church in America .... 1.0 million

Judaism .... 5.9 million

Church of Jesus Christ of L.D.S. (Mormons) .... 3.9 million

Islam .... 3.0 million

Buddhism 100,000

Another way to think about religious identity in the United States is to divide various denominations into specific "families." This is the approach taken in a highly respected assessment of mainline religion in America. Wade Clark Roof and William McKinney identify the following eight groupings:[1]

Liberal Protestants (8.7 percent)
  Episcopalian
  United Church of Christ
  Presbyterian
Moderate Protestants (24.2 percent)
  Methodist
  Lutherans
  Christian (Disciples of Christ)
  Northern Baptist
  Reformed
Conservative Protestants (15.8 percent)
  Southern Baptist

[1] Wade Clark Roof and William McKinney, *American Mainline Religion: Its Changing Shape and Future* (New Brunswick: Rutgers University Press, 1987), pp. 81–99.

Church of Christ
Evangelical/Fundamentalist
Nazarene
Pentecostal/Holiness
Assembly of God
Church of God
Adventist
Black Protestants (9.1 percent)
Methodist
Northern Baptist
Southern Baptist
Catholics (25 percent)
Jews (2.3 percent)
No Religious Preference (6.9 percent)
All Others (8 percent)
Mormon
Jehovah's Witness
Christian Scientist
Unitarian-Universalist

Appendix 2
Using Computers for Analysis

Researchers usually think of computers in connection with statistical analysis, but many people are beginning to find computers extremely helpful in managing bulky field notes that otherwise might have to be recorded in notebooks or laboriously typed and then duplicated and cut apart and filed in various ways. Although at least one software program has been written specifically for field reseachers and various proposals have been made for adapting software not specifically written for field note analysis, any good word-processing program can be used for writing and analyzing field notes.

The following section is intended merely to provide some hints about using computers in your research projects. Most colleges and universities provide access to both instruction and computers for their students. If you have never used a computer, it is unlikely that you will have the time to master its usage simply to complete this assignment. We assume that you have some familiarity with the way a good word-processing program works. Consult the manual for the software program you are using for details.

WHY USE A COMPUTER?

Field work requires a great deal of writing, including long descriptions of events, places, and people, as well as transcription of interviews. The first reason to use a computer is that typing on a computer is much faster than writing field notes by hand or on a typewriter. Beyond the simple fact that it is easier to read something that is typewritten or printed on a computer, word-processing programs provide great flexibility in manipulating a text.

At the simplest level, there are great advantages to being able to change paragraphing and alter spacing and margins. Field notes are often written in a near stream-of-consciousness form. When writing such descriptions (of meetings, buildings, or interactions), one is usually much more interested in getting thoughts down on paper rapidly rather than in perfecting matters of form or sequence.

Word processing not only speeds the process of typing, but it also allows you to go back and put in paragraphs, insert words that were missed, and otherwise make notes more readable. In addition to dividing long sections into paragraphs and straightening out prose, it is easy to insert new headings and subheadings. There is also a considerable advantage to being able to change the margins of field notes easily. You may want to make large right- or left-hand margins so that you can write notes in the margins or code different topics.

At a slightly more complex level, in reading over your field notes, it may seem appropriate to change the order of what you have written. With a word-processing program, it is extremely simple to move a large section of text to another location.

Other features of word processing allow you to treat specific sections of text in ways that make it stand out. You can make text boldface, create a block and underline an entire section, or indent extended quotations or descriptions. And if you want to preserve the original version of your notes, you can easily do so by simply saving subsequent versions of the text under different file names.

ANALYZING FIELD NOTES

So far, we have dealt with the advantages of word processing over written notes. A computer becomes increasingly helpful in the actual process of analyzing the notes. Traditional models of analysis (including the version we have suggested in the text) require duplicate copies, file cards or strips of paper, and multiple file folders. This is a tedious and messy procedure, with different-sized strips of paper and files that must be continually named and renamed. A computer greatly simplifies the analysis process.

While reading through your notes, simply block a sentence, paragraph or section that fits under a particular theme, and then append that block to a file representing the theme. Depending on the extensiveness of your notes, at the end of the project you could have hundreds of such quotations stored neatly in many files, all of them residing on one computer disc.

The process is a little more complex, however, because each quotation must be identified as belonging to a particular interview or observation. Therefore, before blocking the text, simply insert a parenthesis with an identifying code ("March 22, prayer meeting") that allows you to go back and find the context of the quotation.

If you need to file the same quotation under two (or more) separate themes, simply repeat the process and append the same block to both files. The process of blocking and appending is extremely simple and can be done without interrupting the flow of reading through your notes.

One aspect of analyzing field notes is coding and filing them. Another is the process of developing hunches about why things are the way they are, understanding the functions and meanings of certain acts, and ascertaining the significance of certain obervations. Usually these insights will emerge in the process of reading through your notes, and word-processing programs provide several options for registering such insights. You can insert them directly into the text as you proceed, setting them off by boldfacing or underlining; you can use footnotes at the bottom of each page to record such analytical points; or you can create separate files to store insights for future use.

SEARCHES

A helpful feature of most sophisticated programs is their ability to search for key words. This function is very useful in several ways. For example, you can search an entire document for a key word that is commonly associated with an issue or theme; indeed, you could look through all of your files for a concept for which you had not created a separate file. This feature is extremely useful as you accumulate a large or unwieldy amount of data.

A somewhat different application of the search feature is to use it in combination with the search-and-replace function. This is useful especially when working with transcribed interviews when you have guaranteed confidentiality. You can do a literal transcription, and then you can search and replace the proper names (of people, churches, or even communities) with other terms, in order to protect the identity of those who were interviewed and the organization that was studied. Although you may not need to replace such proper names, the search function will allow you to do so if you begin to become uncomfortable about how much you are revealing in your research.

INTERVIEW MANAGEMENT

Word processing can help in other ways in managing interview data. For example, in large interview studies, you may keep lists of who has been interviewed, new prospects to be contacted, and so on. It is very easy to have the computer alphabetize such lists, or to insert new names and omit others, as you proceed.

In addition, if you are writing personalized letters to prospective interviewees, you can save a lot of time by merging names and addresses with a standard letter format. Likewise, if you are sending letters thanking people for their help, you can merge the same list with a letter of appreciation, inserting individualized comments in the letters with little difficulty.

In large interview studies in which you have lists of persons with several key identifying factors (such as ethnicity, denomination, or age), it is easy for the computer to cull lists of people who are distinguished by a particular characteristic (for example, all people over forty years of age).

THE WRITING PROCESS

In many software packages, you can call up two files and either switch back and forth between them, or else have a split screen where they both appear at the same time. This is extremely useful when writing your first draft, because the top of your screen can contain the file from which you are working, and the bottom of the screen can consist of the draft report that you are now writing. You can easily pull quotations from the file and place them in the correct place in your draft.

CONCLUSION

This short introduction to applications of word processing is not a substitute for reading the manual of the program you are using. Nor is this discussion meant to be exhausive of all of the ways in which such programs can be useful to field researchers. But it is clear that computers can play an important role in helping you organize your time and data, and that most of the commonly used programs already have enough built-in functions to make them among the most useful research tools we now possess.

We recognize that many students will not have access to computers, but we urge you to explore the possibilities of buying or borrowing one, or of using your school's computer facilities. Your work will be greatly eased if you can do so.

Appendix 3
Sample Field Notes

What should your field notes look like? How detailed should you make them? How do you put the raw notes taken at your observations into a more organized form? This brief appendix is designed to give you some examples.

Because you may not have attended many religious services, we have structured these notes around a hypothetical observation in a setting with which you are probably extremely familiar: a lecture class in a college course. Although the descriptions provided here will not fit you own experiences, they should give you a good idea of the richness of detail that can be found in an apparently everyday and ordinary event. If you can learn to bring the same degree of perception and openness to your observations in religious settings, you will be on your way to developing a keen sense of the art of social research.

Let us assume, therefore, that the researcher has decided to observe a college lecture, much as you would be expected to observe a religious service of some sort. Our researcher would follow our instructions (provided in Chapters 7 and 8) about preparing for the observation. She finds out that the class session meets at 10 A.M. in a large lecture hall; she arrives fifteen minutes early, in order to get acclimated and to observe the entry process.

The first set of field notes are what you might write down during the visit itself. As you read through the sample field notes that follow, notice in particular the order of the notes and the range of observations included. (Although these notes are typeset, they would of course appear in the researcher's own handwriting on the note pages or cards themselves.)

Field Notes—Rachel Researcher

"Visit to class—Religion 100—March 10, 1988"

Arrive at 9:45; sit down in 10th row.
Room—very large, holds about 150 seats, facing front. Raised lectern in front across entire front wall. Blackboard along front. Windows on left side. Very high ceiling. Hot room, no fans or air cond. Nothing on walls, except a large map of world on right.
Young people wander in slowly, talking to each other. Fill up back seats first, mainly. No one sits in front three rows.
People are evenly split male and female; most white, a few blacks; generally casually dressed, with a few men wearing sports jackets and a few women in skirts or dresses. Most are in jeans or slacks. Hair short. Most carry two or three books.
10:00—older woman enters, goes up to front. Has large pile of books and papers, which she puts on large table next to lectern. She is about 40, long hair, wears a suit, nice shoes, well dressed. Two students go up to her and ask her something. She seems to answer. They sit down. People keep talking around me.
Woman at front begins talking—people get quiet. Most take out a note pad to write in. Woman speaks about how to conduct research in a religious setting—complex task, likely to be hard but rewarding, she says.
Person next to me talks to someone else—distracting to me.
W (woman) walks back and forth across front as she talks.
Most people take notes as she talks.
W—writes on board that "research must be objective, reliable, and valid." Explains each term.
Large clock on wall on right—people occasionally look up at it and check their own watches.
W—paper assignments are due in two months. People look at each other nervously.
My attention begins to wander—hard to concentrate because room is so hot. Some people take off their jackets, roll up sleeves.
W—asks for questions about assignment. No one asks anything. She asks if anyone was paying attention—people laugh.
W—says topic for day is about different versions of Buddhism. Hands out chart (see attached) showing groups. Writes names of groups on board. Some people ask for pronunciation.
People look at chart while she talks, more than at her. Person next to me doodles in his note pad—nothing to do with what she is saying.

Starts raining outside (10:20)—many people start looking out window. W ignores rain—doesn't seem to notice it.

W—gives funny example of Buddhist monk. About a quarter of class laughs. I feel awkward because I am only person in my row laughing. Person next to me looks at me strangely.

W breaks chalk twice in writing on board.

Chairs are very uncomfortable—hard backs, seats too curved. My back hurts. Still very hot. Some people fan themselves with their notebooks.

Walls are white stucco—look quite old, need to be washed.

W—writes more strange words on board. Says people not responsible for knowing them—no one writes them down.

W reads from textbook—about a third of people have the book—they open it and read. Others take notes. W asks what passage means. One man responds. A woman answers next. Another man disagrees with woman. W says points are good.

Person behind me is eating something—can hear crunching and paper opening. Smells like baloney.

I am hungry.

W asks about connection between Buddhist text and Christian Bible. No one says anything. Awkward silence for about fifteen seconds. W answers— defines "scripture" as sacred text, and puts up list of differences.

At 10:40, people start to put notebooks away, and sit starting forward. W looks at watch after a minute or two, and says "That's all for today." Says people should remember quiz next week. Everyone gets up at once and walks out—very noisy. No one talks to W. People leave in groups of three or four. No one talks about Buddhism, that I can hear.

Depending on the purpose of the observation, much more substantive content might have been included in the notes. We have concentrated on a researcher who is interested primarily in the structure and approach of the lecture, rather than on the information communicated by the instructor.

There are several key features of these notes that might help you in your own observations. Notice that the notes are basically in a "stream-of-consciousness" mode. Don't make any effort in your raw field notes to give order to what you see; put down as much as you can as it appears to you. But there is a sort of ordered quality to the notes—for example, "the woman" becomes "W" as it becomes clear that there will be repeated references to her, and each new type of observation is set off in a new paragraph.

In addition, notice the range of types of observations covered in these notes. The researcher has commented about behavior before the class starts, the physical structure of the room, the climate, the attributes of the class, the interaction between students, the physical appearance of the instructor, her lecture style, the topics covered, her interaction with the class, examples of humor and nervousness, inappropriate behavior (such as the person eating), and manner of dismissal. The more precise the researcher was about her research topic, the more observations would have been written down on that particular subject.

What happens with the notes for this one observation? First, the researcher would sit down immediately after the class and write down as many other observations as occurred to her, which she had not written down during the class itself. She would put these on the same piece of paper, but only after drawing a line across the page (or some other form of coding, such as a different color of ink) to distinguish between the two sets of observations.

Depending on whether other observations also take place, a process of transfer and interpretation to a more ordered and usable format would occur next. The transfer could be made onto index cards, other sheets of paper or a computer terminal. The key task would be to separate out key themes. Once again, particular attention would be paid to topics that comprised the central theme of the paper. In addition, interpretive comments would be placed within these notes to spur further thought and provide the basis for the discussion in the paper itself.

Here is what the transferred notes might look like:

Notes—Rachel Researcher

"Transfer re visit to class—Religion 100—March 10, 1988"

Physical nature of room:

> *very large—150 seats, facing front*
> *raised lectern on front*
> *blackboard*
> *windows on left side*
> *very high ceiling*
> *blank walls, except for map on one wall*
> *large clock on wall on right*
> *walls are white stucco, unclean, old*

Climate:
> *very hot*
> *rain outside*
> > *(results in tiredness, hard to concentrate, more informal dress)*

Audience:

> *young—evenly divided between male and female*
> > *most white, few black*
> > *casually dressed, short hair*
> > *most carry books*
> *avoid front rows*

Instructor:

> *Older woman, about 40, long hair, suit, well dressed.*
> *Brings books in with her.*
> *Writes on board, hands out chart, talks most of time, asks some questions, tells a funny story; starts and dismisses class*

Interaction between instructor and others:

> *Some talk to her before class—they come up to her*
> *She asks occasional questions—usually no answer*
> *She asks what passage means.*
> *She answers her own questions when no one else does.*

Atmosphere:

> *Most people listen—some talk, one eats. (Distracting)*
> *Some look at clock and check watches (sign of inattention?)*
> *People nervous about future assignment, when mentioned.*
> *(Heat affects concentration and attitude.)*
> *Some humor—about not paying attention, about funny story. (Breaks ice? Establishes relationship with class? Shows funny side of Buddhism?)*

Other comments:

> *Instructor seems less aware of rain outside than do others (she is concentrating more?)*
> *My awkwardness because I laugh (and because I don't know anyone?)*
> *People don't write down things when they are told they don't have to know them (why??)*

If the transfer is being performed to note cards, each of the themes would appear on a different card. In either case, notice how observations from different parts of the original notes are grouped under a single heading. Some phrases are shortened, some expanded, and some ignored if found to be redundant or irrelevant.

The parenthetical comments are especially important, because they begin the interactive process of thinking through what the observations mean. Sometimes multiple interpretations are listed for future consideration; at other times, questions are raised with no obvious interpretation in sight. The point is to put the notes into a form that can then serve as the foundation for the analysis stage of the research, as well as to suggest other observations that need to be performed in the course of the research.

Index

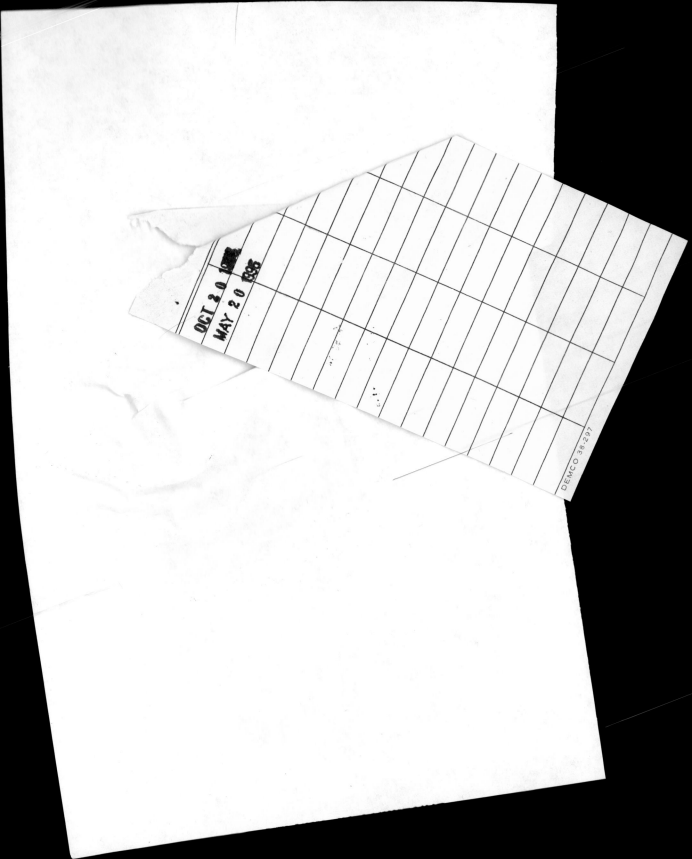

DEMCO 38-297